MARLON K. HOM

Songs of
Gold Mountain

CANTONESE RHYMES FROM
SAN FRANCISCO CHINATOWN

University of California Press
BERKELEY · LOS ANGELES · LONDON

This book is a print-on-demand volume. It is manufactured using toner in place of ink. Type and images may be less sharp than the same material seen in traditionally printed University of California Press editions.

University of California Press
Berkeley and Los Angeles, California

University of California Press, Ltd.
London, England

© 1987 by The Regents of the University of California

First Paperback Printing 1992

An abridged version of the second half of the introductory essay appeared in *Western Folklore* (1983); song 16 appeared in *Amerasia Journal* (1982); songs 2-9, 11, 12, 14, and 16 appeared in *Greenfield Review* (1983) Renditions of these rhymes are slightly different in the present volume.

Library of Congress Cataloging-in-Publication Data

Chin-shan ko chi. English.
    Songs of Gold Mountain.

    Translation of: Chin-shan ko chi.
    1. Chinese poetry—California—San Francisco—Translations into English. 2. English poetry—Translations from Chinese. 3. Chinese poetry—California—San Francisco. 4. Chinese poetry—20th century. 5. China—Emigration and immigration—Poetry. 6. California—Emigration and immigration—Poetry. 7. Chinatown (San Francisco, Calif.)—Poetry. I. Hom, Marlon K. II. Title.
PL3164.5.E5C54   1987   895.1'1   86-11234
ISBN 0-520-08104-8

Printed in the United States of America

*Songs of
Gold Mountain*

倉山歌集

Contents

Acknowledgments

In the course of doing research on Chinese American literature, I came across a "Wooden Barracks" poem at the Angel Island Immigration Station, written by a Cantonese immigrant sometime between 1910 and 1930. I have translated it as follows:

> Poems, thousands and thousands, written all
>   over the walls:
> All words of grievances and sorrow.
> Should we one day be freed from this prison,
>   and prosper with success,
> Treasure the memory: marks of all those years.

Times have changed considerably in the last fifty years. Still, the literature of the Chinese in America prior to the 1950s remains largely unknown even to many Chinese Americans today. Books by recent Chinese American writers promoted by American publishers have gained their deserved recognition and acceptance, but the literature of the early Chinese Americans is still buried in the past. It was not until very recently that the poems of the Chinese immigrants on Angel Island became known and were translated into English, allowing us to understand and appreciate in depth a chapter of our literary heritage.

I hope that the present work, a selection of Cantonese vernacular rhymes from San Francisco Chinatown, written in the early 1910s, will be still another window into early Chinese American literary life, and that it will provide us with authentic knowledge of the experiences of Chinese in America at the turn of this century.

For this volume, I am especially grateful to Mr. Him Mark Lai of the Chinese Historical Society of America in San Francisco. Mark Lai, as he is usually called, is the dean of Chinese American history and has been most generous in sharing his vast knowledge and huge collection of Chinese American materials. My casual inquiry to him about early Chinatown literature resulted in his providing me, from his own library, with photocopies of the rare *Jinshan ge ji* (Songs of Gold Mountain) anthologies of 1911 and 1915. Among teachers and friends who have read my manuscript, in part or in its entirety, and have offered me valuable criticism and suggestions for revision, I am especially thankful to Professors Wu-chi Liu and Jeffery P. Chan, Frank Chin, Russell Leong, Ruthanne McCunn, and Sam Solberg. Mr. Tan Bi-yon also gave me additional insights for the revision of my manuscript during our two meetings in San Francisco in April 1984. Lorraine has been working with me on the Chinese American literature project untiringly all these years; her support has been unrelenting. Dr. Barbara Metcalf, Ms. Phyllis Killen, and Ms. Susan Stone, editors at the University of California Press, and Ms. Sally Serafim have given me tremendous assistance and expert advice in preparing this volume for publication. Of course, I alone am responsible for all the imperfection in this book.

Translator's Note

All Cantonese expressions are transcribed in a modified Yale Cantonese romanization system. A Mandarin equivalent in *pinyin* transcription is given in parentheses. E.g.: Gamsaan (Jinshan) for Gold Mountain.

There are two sets of footnotes to the rhymes. The notes to the Chinese originals consist of a collation of misused homophonous words; wrong words are cited and correct ones appended. Regional Cantonese expressions are annotated in standard Chinese. The notes to the translations provide annotation to Chinese literary expressions that are not self-explanatory in English.

Abbreviations: JSGJ I: *Jinshan ge ji* (1911)
JSGJ II: *Jinshan ge erji* (1915)

The Songs of
Gold Mountain

An Introduction to
Cantonese Vernacular Rhymes from
San Francisco Chinatown

Early Chinatown: A Historical Overview

ESTABLISHING THE OLDEST
AMERICAN CHINATOWN

The French sinologist M. de Guignes wrote in 1761 that
the Chinese had first come to the American continent
one thousand years before the European explorers,
when Hui Shen, a Buddhist monk, came to a land called
Fusang, which de Guignes identified as the west coast of
North America. Upon returning to China, Hui Shen
reported in detail on the livelihood of the Fusang na-
tives. His account appears in the sixth-century A.D. his-
torical text *Liang shu*.[1] However, no other conclusive

1. French Sinologist M. de Guignes's study was based on the
account in volume 54 of the *Liang shu* (History of the Liang dynasty),
a historical work written between 502 and 556. Some later scholars
rejected this study, or tried to identify "Fusang" as another place. A
brief summary regarding this issue and further references are given
in Thomas Chin et al., *A History of Chinese in California* (San Fran-
cisco: Chinese Historical Society of America, 1969), pp. 1–2.

documents are available on this so-called early discovery of America by the Chinese. Recent Chinese anthropological studies have, however, drawn comparisons between the Chinese and the natives of America, showing some similarities in language and culture between the two peoples now separated by the Pacific Ocean.[2]

The verifiable Chinese presence in America came much later. In the mid-seventeenth century, Chinese seamen traveled on board Spanish trading vessels via the Philippine Islands, which were known in Cantonese as Leuisung (Lüsong), after the island of Luzon. Some settled in Mexico, which they called Siu Leuisung (Xiao Lüsong) or Little Luzon, probably because Spanish was spoken in both countries and they thus appeared similar in culture. These Chinese settlers became a part of the local community, making their living among the Mexicans.[3] Merchants and traders from southeastern China,

2. Wei Juxian, *Zhongguoren faxian Meizhou chu kao* (A preliminary investigation on the Chinese discovery of America) (Taibei: Shishi chuban gongsi, 1975). Wei uses archaeological evidence of similarities between Native American and Chinese culture to suggest that Native Americans are Chinese in origin. See also Wei's *Zhongguoren faxian Meizhou tiyao* (A summary regarding the Chinese discovery of America) (Rpt., Taibei: Shishi chuban gongsi, 1975) in which he claims that ancient China had a long history of communication with natives in the American continent. *Fusang* is often identified as a hibiscus plant. In Chinese writings, its red blossom alludes to the sun, hence it becomes the name for the eastern part of the world where the sun rises and, consequently, for the island nation of Japan, which literally means "sun's origin." However, Wei in his studies argues that *fusang* must be the redwoods of America. He also cites the mention of hummingbirds, native birds of America that never appeared in any Chinese writings prior to that entry in the *Liang shu*, as proof of his theory, since it was Hui Shen who introduced these new items to China.

3. Chin et al., p. 6.

long experienced in doing business with foreigners,
were seen regularly in the ports of Mexico. In 1838 the
earliest Chinese reached Yerba Buena, the name for San
Francisco before California was incorporated into the
United States in 1850.[4]

In 1849, the news of the discovery of gold in Califor-
nia reached China, and hundreds of Chinese began ar-
riving in the early months of 1850. Thousands followed
in subsequent years, as mining, farming, and railroad
construction boomed. Then, as now, the Chinese called
the United States Gamsaan (Jinshan), or Gold Moun-
tain, a term deriving from the 1849 Gold Rush. It was
also called Fakei (Huaqi), or Flowery Flag, a name
inspired by the fancy graphics of the American flag.

Instead of the cruel coolie system of slavery found in
Southeast Asia and South America, the Chinese workers
usually came to the United States under the "credit
fare" system. A man would repay the loan that paid
his passage by working under contract for a specified
period. He was then free to pursue his own living.
Workers were largely Cantonese, natives of Guangdong
province in southeastern China, an area that had pros-
pered from foreign trade since the sixteenth century.
Specifically, they came from two regions around the
Pearl River delta. The Saamyup (Sanyi) area consisted
of the "Three Counties"—Naamhoi (Nanhai), Punyu
(Panyu), and Seundak (Shunde). The Seiyup (Siyi) area
encompassed the "Four Counties" of Sunning (Xin-
ning)/Toisaan (Taishan), Sunwui (Xinhui), Hoiping
(Kaiping), and Yanping (Enping). Saamyup natives in

4. Chin et al., p. 10. In 1946, Americans renamed Yerba Buena
"San Francisco."

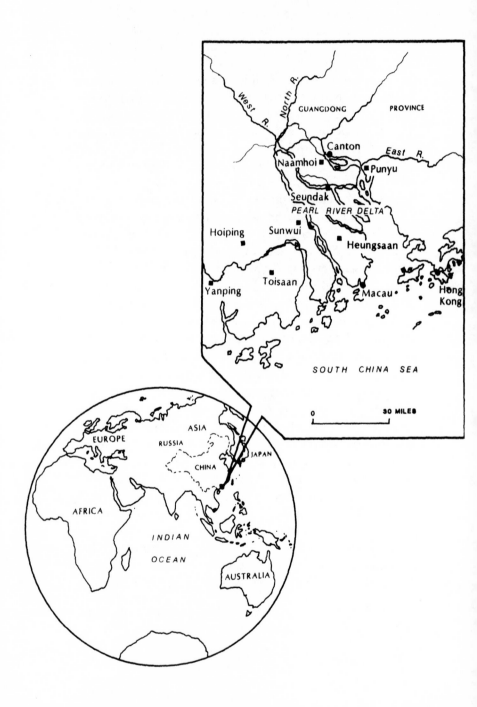

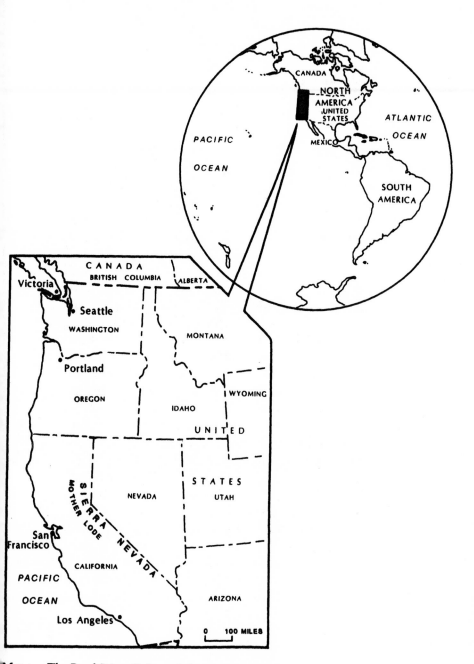

Map 1. The Pearl River Delta and the American West Coast

America often engaged in mercantile and other business trades; Seiyup natives, mainly laborers, accounted for 70 percent of the total Chinese population in the United States.[5]

In San Francisco, the Chinese soon formed fraternal organizations based on their county of origin to assist those who came to earn a living in America. In the early 1850s, most Chinese workers did not stay long in the port. For them, as for their white Gold Rush counterparts, San Francisco was only a stopover on the way to the vast interior. Merchants, traders, and providers of services and supplies would stay. In the mid-1850s, more Chinese began to settle in San Francisco, engaging in service industries, which provided stable employment and income. The so-called Chinatown of San Francisco was formed in those early years, as a concentrated area of Chinese commercial and other business operations began to take shape. The owners and workers usually occupied living quarters located behind the storefronts. However, Chinese were scattered throughout this frontier city, living an integrated existence among San Franciscans of various ethnic and cultural origins.

At first, the arrival in California of the "China boys" was welcomed. Aside from working in the mines, the Chinese provided the major labor force for reclaiming California land for farming. Some were skilled fishermen and shrimp harvesters. Later, tens of thousands worked, and many died, building the transcontinental railroad, even laying a record-breaking ten miles of track in a single day on April 28, 1869. However, by the mid-1850s, conflicts had developed in the mines, and

5. Chin et al., p. 4.

Chinese miners became the victims. When the transcontinental railroads were completed in 1869, a massive labor surplus was created. Some Chinese workers left for the farms, but many turned to San Francisco, now the major urban center in the West. However, the railroad was also facilitating the movement of workers from the depressed East Coast cities into an already saturated West. Conflicts arose, fueled by the belief in "manifest destiny" by the white men who would claim the American continent. This created a tremendous hardship for the Chinese on the West Coast, who became the objects of attack by and exclusion from the greater American society. The benign tolerance of times past turned into hysterical rejection. "The Chinese must go!" became an accepted slogan, serving the self-interest of both the white working class and the opportunistic politicians, as wealthy capitalists exploited cheap Chinese labor for their own gain.[6] Chinese were attacked everywhere as white workingmen and labor unionists and their supporters tried to drive the Chinese away.

California had the largest concentration of Chinese; many lived in San Francisco. Although discriminatory practices were severe in the city, there was no safer or economically more feasible place for them to go. The Chinese realized that the presence of so many of their countrymen would enable them to render mutual as-

6. For an excellent analysis of the conflict in the triangular relationship among the white working class and white unionists, the capitalists, and the Chinese workers, see Alexander Saxton, *The Indispensable Enemy: Labor and the Anti-Chinese Movement in California* (Berkeley: University of California Press, 1971). Saxton views labor conflicts between the Chinese and white workers from a class perspective, in which the capitalists manipulate the two groups to advance their self-interest and their profits.

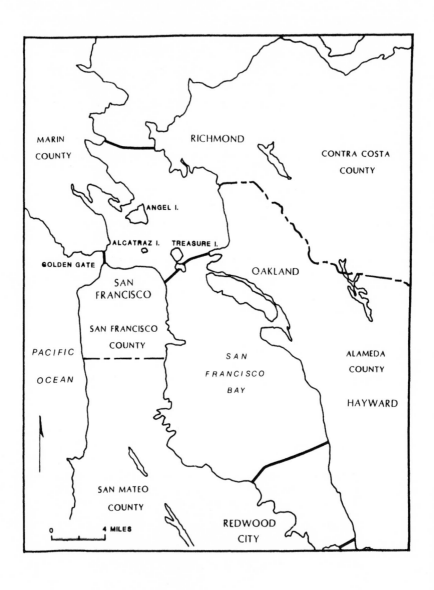

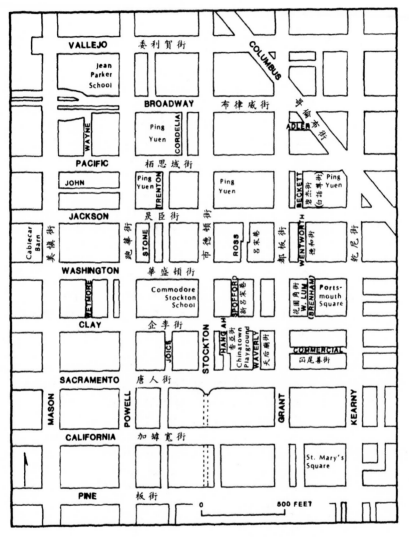

Map 2. San Francisco Bay Area, with Street Map of Chinatown

sistance and comfort in a time of crisis. As it turned out, while the Chinese were often stoned or physically abused in non-Chinese neighborhoods, once inside their own enclave they were relatively safe. As a result, a large Chinese community, sometimes called the "Canton of the West," existed in San Francisco by the early 1870s. It was located two blocks west of Yerba Buena Cove, the city harbor (today the landfilled area occupied by the financial district and the Embarcadero). The area surrounding Portsmouth Plaza (now Portsmouth Square) and Dupont Street (now Grant Avenue, but in Chinese still called by its former name) was San Francisco's downtown, but later, when Chinese businesses and residents moved in as white ones moved out, it became part of Chinatown. Sacramento Street was called Tongyan gaai (Tangren jie), the Street of the Chinese. By the time the Chinese Exclusion Act of 1882 restricting Chinese immigration was passed, the Chinese population in America had reached 132,000.[7] Nearly 10 percent of San Francisco's 1880 population of 233,959 were Chinese.[8]

San Francisco Chinatown became well established as its residents grew to represent an integral part of the work force of the city. They were dominant in industries like shoe making and shirt and cigar manufacturing, and in service industries like the laundry business. Meanwhile, the trans-Pacific mercantile trade provided Chinatown with goods that were not otherwise available in America. Well-defined social organizations were established in Chinatown through clan, district, and fraternal affiliations, all of which were governed by a

7. Chin et al., p. 18.
8. Chin et al., p. 21.

supreme joint administration known as the Six Companies (later the Consolidated Chinese Benevolent Association). Where the San Francisco city and other government agencies failed, the Six Companies maintained and protected the welfare and interests of the Chinese residents. After the 1906 earthquake and fire completely destroyed Chinatown, efforts were made to move Chinatown from the downtown area bordered by Kearny, Stockton, California, and Broadway to a remote southeastern corner of the city. However, the attempt failed and the Chinese returned to the old site to rebuild among the ruins.

The Chinese population in the United States began to drop as the Exclusion Act was enforced. Because of the numerous discriminatory immigration laws and local ordinances of the ensuing years, many Chinese already in America were unable to stay on. They were not allowed to become naturalized citizens, nor could they own land. In California, interracial sex and marriage were prohibited. San Francisco's Chinatown was frequently raided, and Chinese residents caught without proper identification were arrested and often deported unless they could prove they were legal immigrants. U.S. immigration officials often denied re-entry even to Chinese travelers with valid re-entry certificates, on grounds that their documents had been invalidated by new immigration regulations. The Chinese regularly challenged the many unfair laws in courts. Even so, by 1900, the U.S. census reported a drop in the Chinese population to less than 90,000; by 1910, to 71,531; and by 1920, to 61,639—about one-half of the reported figure in 1882.

Despite the abundance of exclusionary laws, many Chinese nevertheless found ways to circumvent them.

Crossing the border from Mexico was one common practice. The 1906 San Francisco earthquake and fire, moreover, gave the Chinese an immigration reprieve. Official birth records had been destroyed by the fire, and many Chinese oldtimers in San Francisco took the opportunity to claim citizenship, saying that their American birth records had been destroyed. This opened up a new avenue for the younger generation, who could then claim to be the foreign-born, unmarried children of American citizens, a category unaffected by the exclusionary laws. Actually, many of the oldtimers had married shortly before coming, and had left their brides in China. Another practice was to come as a "paper son," assuming a false identity and claiming to be the offspring of an American citizen.[9] As the early Chinese population was overwhelmingly Cantonese, the immigrants who came through these methods were from the same Cantonese locale. Hence, the Saamyup and Seiyup population distribution in America did not dramatically change, although the Seiyup immigrants, being mostly laborers, were the major target of the exclusion.

9. Him Mark Lai et al. briefly explain the "paper son" practice as follows: (1) a Chinese with United States citizenship rights would return from China and report the birth in China of a child, usually a son, thus creating an immigration slot for the newborn; (2) the slot would be sold to a relative, friend, or even a stranger through a broker (price in 1930 was $100 per age year; thus, a slot for a seventeen-year-old would cost $1,700); (3) the paper son would be coached on his immigration testimony in preparation for his interrogation upon arrival to the United States. See Him Mark Lai et al., *Outline of the History of the Chinese in America* (San Francisco: by the authors, 1971), p. 96. All newcomers and returnees to America were meticulously interrogated by immigration officials. Like anyone else, paper sons who failed would be denied entry and deported back to China. Usually, a bribe was one recourse to ensure safe passage through United States immigration.

Nevertheless, the Chinese population in America survived, despite everything. Discrimination only served to fortify the independence of the Chinese community and to make racial differences all the more apparent in the greater American society. Contrary to the claim of many critics in the past, the formation of San Francisco Chinatown was not just a result of the Chinese immigrants' unwillingness to assimilate. Nor was it formed merely as the product of the Chinese immigrants' desire to preserve their own way of life. Part of the historical basis for its emergence can be found in the Chinese response to racism. Chinatown was created as a means of survival during a time of rampant racial intolerance, when the Chinese were forced to retreat from an integrated existence to an alienated one. Chinatown's independent internal social structure resulted from social injustices from without, as experience showed that the Chinese could not depend on local laws, which discriminated against them and perpetuated their hardship. Chinatown had to establish itself and prosper on its own for the survival of its inhabitants.

LITERARY DEPICTIONS OF CHINATOWN LIFE

Although San Francisco Chinatown was always viewed as an ethnic Chinese enclave, a "city within a city," its street life was actually "vibrant with a curious and colorful mix of Chinese and non-Chinese," with its stores displaying goods to be consumed by Chinese and non-Chinese alike.[10] Chinatown's inhabitants were ac-

10. John Kuo Wei Tchen, *Arnold Genthe's Photographs of San Francisco's Old Chinatown* (New York: Dover Publications, 1984), p. 19.

tively engaged in making a living, just like other hard-working San Franciscans.[11] They worked in factories adjacent to Chinatown; they managed their own businesses and peddled their goods and wares. The Chinese community, though fearful of white man's intrusion and disruption, was open to exploration and observation by non-Chinese. Some whites even became Chinatown tour guides, creating a picture of an exotic, mysterious Chinatown for tourists by hiring poor souls to display their bound feet or smoke opium. A tremendous quantity of writings on the Chinese and Chinatown, most of it critical and negative, appeared in local newspapers and in the influential *Overland Monthly*, a local publication whose contributors were recognized American writers from the West.

Writings appearing after the 1880s tended to depict Chinatown in an extremely negative light, appealing to fears of the "Yellow Peril," the white man's xenophobic fear of Asians. The emphasis was on Chinatown as a foreign and exotic place, thus perpetuating its mystery. As Alexander McLeod later found in his studies of the early Chinese in America, the non-Chinese regarded San Francisco Chinatown as "mysterious" and totally "different."[12] American frontier writers, including Jack London, wrote about the Chinese with bias and distortion based upon an unfounded fear that an onslaught of

11. Liu Boji, *Meiguo Huaqiao shi* (*A history of the Chinese in the United States of America, 1848–1911*) (Taibei: Liming wenhua shiye gongsi, 1976), pp. 106–7. (Hereafter cited as *History*.)

12. Alexander McLeod, *Gold Dust and Pigtails* (Caldwell, Ida.: The Caxton Printers, 1949). McLeod describes mysterious and exotic practices of San Francisco Chinatown since the 1850s. Chapter 10 (pp. 268–81), for example, describes Chinatown as a "different world" from the white America.

Chinese would conquer America.[13] The literary hysteria fanned the flames for stricter laws to exclude the Chinese. On the other hand, a few writers were less prejudiced. Mark Twain called the Chinese "harmless," and said they should be left alone.[14] Francis Bret Harte was of the opinion that the Chinese were wise and could not easily be taken in by white men's trickery.[15] However, most popular writers in the pulp genre engaged in vicious muckraking, depicting Chinatown as a sinful, foreign, crime-ridden ghetto.

Amidst these negative and distorted treatments, the works of Arnold Genthe (1869–1942) and Edith Eaton (1867–1914) stand out for their fair treatment of the authentic Chinatown. They were able to capture the vivid and vibrant livelihood of Chinatown in the late 1890s and the early 1900s, because they were actively present in the community and knew Chinatown resi-

13. William P. Fenn, in *Ah Sin and His Brethren in American Literature* (Peking: College of Chinese Studies, 1933), provides the first critical analysis of the Chinese in American literature, showing how the Chinese are often portrayed as foreigners, in a very negative light. Limin Chu's *The Image of China and the Chinese in the Overland Monthly, 1868–1875, 1883–1935* (Duke University, Ph.D. dissertation, 1965), gives details on xenophobic writings published in San Francisco since 1870. William F. Wu, in his *Yellow Peril: Chinese Americans in American Fiction, 1850–1940* (Hamden, Conn.: Archon Books, 1982), also shows how American writers, including the "local colorists" of the West, created a villainous image of the Chinese in America with racist distortions and stereotypes. Such writings catered to a popular demand to perpetuate the image of Chinatown as mysterious and foreign as well as crime-ridden. None gave a valid, objective portrayal of the Chinese way of life in Chinatown.

14. Mark Twain, *Roughing It* (New York: New American Library, 1962), pp. 291–97.

15. Francis Bret Harte, "Plain Language from Truthful James," *Overland Monthly* 5, no. 2 (September 1870): 287–88.

dents personally. Genthe recorded and preserved the life and images of Chinatown in his photographs;[16] Eaton did so in a score of short stories whose protagonists were Chinatown residents.[17] Genthe's photographs of Chinatown before the 1906 disaster showed its bustling street scenes, telling a lively pictorial story of its men, women, and children. Edith Eaton, under the pen name of Sui Sin Far, depicted the trials and tribulations of Chinatown families as they tried to establish homes in America. She also effectively probed behind the laughter and tears of contact between the Chinatown residents and the white majority. Both artists, in their respective media, captured a true-life picture of Chinatown that was rarely depicted by other American artists of the time.

CHINATOWN LOW LIFE:
THE THREE VICES

Racial intolerance and xenophobic practices have accounted for most of the negative depictions of China-

16. See John Tchen's introduction to *Arnold Genthe's Photographs of San Francisco's Old Chinatown*, pp. 3–18. Genthe published his photographs first in *Pictures of Old Chinatown* (New York: Moffat, Yard, and Co., 1908) and again in *Old Chinatown: A Book of Pictures* (New York: Mitchell Kennerly, 1913). Because the old Chinatown was destroyed in the 1906 earthquake and fire, Genthe's photographs are most valuable today to the study of old Chinatown. John Tchen's 1984 publication provides an excellent explanation and analysis of these photographs.

17. Sui Sin Far (Edith Eaton), *Mrs. Spring Fragrance* (Chicago: A. C. McClurg, 1912). The short stories that are particularly of interest in dealing with family and social life in Chinatown during the late 1890s and early 1900s are "The Wisdom of the New" (pp. 47–85), "Its Wavering Image" (pp. 85–95), "The Story of One White Woman Who Married a Chinese" and "Her Chinese Husband" (pp. 111–44), "The Americanizing of Pau Tsu" (pp. 144–61), and "In the Land of the Free" (pp. 161–78).

town life since the 1880s. No one could deny that Chinatown was different, nor that it had its share of serious social problems in a society that accepted and practiced racial discrimination and segregation. Chinatown was criticized particularly for its social vices—prostitution, opium addiction, and gambling. It was frequently attacked as a place of filth and sin, whose values were in direct contradiction to the Christian ethics so valued by white American society.

However, if viewed objectively, the vices of early San Francisco Chinatown seem no worse or more malicious than the vices of any other frontier town in the West during that period. Ever since the Gold Rush days, prostitution had prospered throughout San Francisco. Mining and railroad construction work encouraged a tremendous influx of male workers to the West, but the migratory nature of the work discouraged most of them from establishing normal family lives. Prostitution was recognized as a necessity and was in full operation wherever there were a large number of male workers. As the center of the West, ever since the 1850s San Francisco's downtown district was littered with houses of ill repute, some of which were more "reputable" than others based on the reputability of their clientele. At first, the prostitutes came from various Caucasian backgrounds. Soon, Chinese and Japanese prostitutes also appeared. Only Chinatown's proximity to downtown and the existence of a separate Chinese operation in Chinatown made it a part of that infamous scene.

Ever since the early period of immigration, prostitution had been a community concern in Chinatown, since Chinese women often were prevented from coming to America and Chinese men were denied the

opportunity to live a normal family life in America.[18]
The sex ratio of the Chinese population in San Francisco
was extremely imbalanced. At its worst, in 1880, there
were only 1,781 Chinese women in a Chinese popula-
tion of 21,745.[19] Predictably, this sex ratio provided a
favorable climate for the emergence in 1852 of Hip Yee
Tong, a fraternal group that engaged in a profitable
operation, importing Chinese women from China to
be prostitutes. Thousands were brought over by the
organization, which came to monopolize the traffic. In
the beginning, some prostitutes came voluntarily on
their own. Later, young girls and women in their teens
were brought over and groomed for the business, most
coming from impoverished families that had sold them
to agents operating in China. Many were victims of
kidnapping and other means of deceit and enticement.[20]
One recent point of view holds prostitution to be a form
of labor, in which women offer their sexuality in ex-
change for a fee,[21] but what went on was hardly the
same as male workers offering their labor and strength
to earn a wage. Life for these Chinese women, com-
monly known as "slave girls," was cruel and inhu-
mane.[22] They were treated like merchandise, often sold
and resold many times. Societal attitudes stripped away
their self-respect and pride. A few lucky ones were pur-

18. Lucie Cheng, "Free, Indentured, Enslaved: Chinese Pros-
titutes in Nineteenth-Century America," in *Labor Immigration under
Capitalism: Asian Workers in the United States before World War II*, ed.
Lucie Cheng and Edna Bonacich (Berkeley: University of Califor-
nia Press, 1984), pp. 405–6.

19. Mary Coolidge, *Chinese Immigration* (1909; rpt., New York:
Arno Press, 1969), p. 502; and Chin et al., p. 21.

20. Cheng, pp. 407–08.

21. Ibid., pp. 424–25.

22. McLeod, pp. 173–86.

chased by the rich and powerful as mistresses or con-
cubines. Most, however became diseased by their pro-
fession and were often left to die in the most pathetic
way, without human dignity.

The importation of prostitutes was prohibited by law
in 1873, but many still landed in America through ille-
gal means. Anti-Asian groups in San Francisco criti-
cized Chinatown for its prostitution. Reform efforts
from within Chinatown failed to halt Hip Yee Tong's
ruthless activity, however, as the latter enjoyed the law's
protection and collaboration through bribery.[23] Never-
theless, prostitution declined city-wide after the 1900s,
when Victorian Christians reaching San Francisco active-
ly moved to transform this once freewheeling frontier
city into a metropolis of stable families and industrial
growth.[24] White missionary women in Chinatown,
led by Margaret Culbertson and later by Donaldina
Cameron, were able to "rescue" many slave girls and
provide shelter for those who fled from their owners.
These missionaries were successful mainly because, like
most Chinese in the early days, the Hip Yee Tong
avoided getting involved in disputes with Caucasians
unless it was absolutely necessary. The Hip Yee Tong
might go after the Chinese who helped the prostitutes
escape, but not Caucasians. Hundreds of Chinese women
were able to lead a normal life as a result of Donaldina
Cameron's tireless rescue efforts. Her accomplishment
won praises but at the same time overdramatized the
problem of prostitution in Chinatown. The focus on
prostitution in Chinatown, in a city where the immoral
trade was rampant, also revealed the "paternalistic atti-

23. Liu Boji, *History*, pp. 128–30.
24. Cheng, pp. 423–24.

tude" of the white missionaries and their "racial hypocrisy," [25] and contributed to the concerted attack on the Chinese. White houses of prostitution just around the corner tended to be ignored, however. The missionary attitude tended to perpetuate white supremacist attitudes and strengthen the already negative image of the "heathen Chinese" in America during a period of hysterical exclusion.

Opium was equally targeted for attack. This potent drug was brought to southern China in large quantities by the British merchants of the East India Company, the very same company involved in the Boston Tea Party. Opium smoking was a lethal addiction, but it was passed off as something healthful. British merchants and their agents in China promoted opium, a product of the British colony of India, as an elixir of life, a cure-all. As addiction became widespread in Guangdong province, it created epidemic social disorder, with addicts wasting away their lives and bringing ruin to their families. An all-out campaign to eradicate the import in the late 1830s failed, only giving the British imperialists an excuse to champion their "gunboat diplomacy." Britain won the infamous Opium War of 1840, colonized Hong Kong, and expanded her opium trade in China. As a result, opium addiction took its toll on the Chinese population. The Japanese would later call the Chinese "the sick men of Asia" because of the withered physiques of addicts in the Chinese coastal cities.

British promotion of opium smoking made it an acceptable social pastime among the Chinese. Many deeply believed in its medicinal power. For a long time, the habit was regarded highly as a privilege of the elite

25. Tchen, p. 96.

class. The Cantonese immigrants brought the habit with them to America, since there were no specific regulations on the substance prior to the 1860s. In 1869, the Burlingame Treaty between China and the United States prohibited the Chinese in America from importing opium. However, the treaty did not stop the import of the drug through non-Chinese operations. Opium came from Hong Kong through the Fook Hing Company, a company that served as a refiner and distributor for the British, and the customs house in San Francisco levied a hefty tariff on it. This duty-paid substance, known as *gung yin* (*gong yan*), "taxed opium," was packaged in tins the size of sardine cans and sold openly in San Francisco Chinatown.[26]

It is said that over two hundred opium dens once operated in San Francisco Chinatown, many of them shady operations located in basements and tiny alleyways.[27] They were considered by white Americans to be the most disgusting sight in Chinatown.[28] Their existence testified to the gloomy side of the Chinese immigrant way of life. The small, crowded opium dens were usually dimly lit; the walls were black with years of smoke; the thick air was totally smoke-filled. In them addicts lay sideways on crudely prepared beds, busying themselves with the chemical substance and the smoking apparatus, silently puffing away their savings, their families, and finally their own lives.

26. McLeod, p. 155. For a detailed study of the opiate problems in the United States, see David T. Courtwright, *Dark Paradise: Opiate Addiction in America before 1940* (Cambridge, Mass.: Harvard University Press, 1982); pages 62–86 cover the situation in San Francisco at the turn of the century.

27. Liu Boji, *History*, p. 120.

28. McLeod, p. 156.

City officials paid little attention to the opium addiction in Chinatown, which they regarded as primarily a Chinese problem that did not affect the white population.[29] Later, however, as whites became addicts and as opium dens catering solely to white patrons sprouted on California and Pine streets, the local authorities became alarmed. By the 1880s, opium addiction was a citywide issue, and the Chinese were blamed for it. Local ordinances were passed to control and punish operators and patrons of opium dens.[30] However, the drug was still sold openly and the customs house still collected a hefty duty annually on its import.

In 1909, federal laws were passed to ban the import of opium. As supplies dwindled, the price soared, from $12 per pound to $70 in 1917.[31] As a result, smuggling and bribery became the norm in the attempts to bring in the drug. The shortage, the price hikes, and the possibility of criminal prosecution, coupled with a vigorous campaign to eradicate opium addiction in Chinatown, brought about its eventual demise.

The popularity of opium smoking during this period had its roots in the fact that the Cantonese had long been exposed to the drug and accepted it as they did tobacco smoking. Their life in America—an abnormal existence punctuated with hardship, loneliness, and alienation— and the availability of the drug in the open market only led more people to the drug as they tried to seek solace by means of a temporary escape. However, the Cantonese had also witnessed the destruction of their homeland in the Opium War of 1840, which sowed hatred

29. Liu Boji, *History*, p. 120.
30. Ibid., p. 121.
31. Ibid., p. 122; also Courtwright, p. 83.

toward the drug among Cantonese intellectuals. Some came to America and, in local Chinese newspapers, advocated a ban on opium long before the United States passed that law in 1909. Not one piece of Chinatown writing can be found in support or defense of opium smoking. However, for nearly sixty years after the massive Chinese immigration began, American authorities allowed the import and sale of opium and regarded it as only a Chinese problem, forgetting that the problem had originally been brought about by the British imperialists. It is disheartening to note that the ills of opium addiction, which inflicted so much misery for so long on San Francisco Chinatown, were ignored and nothing was done until it finally started to take its toll on the Caucasian population.

Finally, there was gambling. Man's interest in games of chance is universal, and Chinese immigrants, like their European counterparts, brought their favorite games with them to America. Gambling, like alcohol and prostitutes, was a fixture of the saloons of Western frontier towns. However, since the Chinese could not patronize the white man's saloons at the time, they had their own gambling operations in their own community. These establishments were also frequented by Caucasians, Filipinos, Japanese, and other ethnic groups.

Many Chinese games of chance were popular in America in the early period.[32] The most famous were *faantaan* (*fantan*), literally, "turn over the display," *baakgaap piu* (*baige piao*), literally "pigeon's note" but better known as the "Chinese lottery," *paaigau* (*paijiu*), or

---

32. See Stewart Culin, *The Gambling Games of the Chinese in America* (1891; rpt. Las Vegas: Gambler's Book Club, 1982).

"arrange in nine" but better known as "Chinese dominoes," and mahjong—all games that are still played today. Mahjong, a time-consuming game, is a kind of clubhouse game played more for socializing than for gambling, as seen in the Chinese American novel *Eat a Bowl of Tea* (1962) by Louis Chu, and has become popular with some segments of the Jewish community.

Among all ethnic groups, the most popular games of chance were the simple games. For example, *faantaan* is simply a game of elementary counting. An unknown number of Chinese coins are covered by a bowl, and players bet on four numbers, one to four, or on "even" or "odd." After all bets have been placed, the dealer removes the bowl and quickly counts off the coins with a chopstick, counting four coins at a time, until four or less remain. For example, if two remain, bets on "two" and "even" would be the winners. The game's apparatus can be improvised easily. Instead of coins, beans can be used. Hence, the game was very popular at work camps during the early days. The Japanese laborers' indulgence in this Chinese game of chance was immense.[33]

Baakgaap piu is a lottery game based on the first eighty words of the "Thousand Word Prose" (*Qian zi wen*), a well-known four-word-per-line prose-poem. No words are duplicated in the prose; hence there are eighty different spots on which the players can bet. A player wins if his choice of word(s) matches the winning word(s). Two lotteries were held each day by each operator in San Francisco Chinatown, one at noon and one in the evening. The game's popularity was due to the fact that, in addition to being a simple lottery that required no skill

33. Liu Boji, *History*, p. 120.

but only luck, it did not require presence of the player, who could carry on his usual business while playing the game. Agents in storefronts wrote up the lottery tickets for the players; in addition, couriers for the operators were readily available to pick up or deliver bets and winnings. This game was also well received by non-Chinese players. The Japanese mockingly called it *baka* ("foolish"), a play on its Chinese name, *baakgap* (lit., "pigeon"). It was also immensely popular among white players, so much so that, according to Stewart Culin, white casinos later adopted it and turned it into the game of Race Horse Keno, and later, simply Keno.[34] Here, eighty numbers, written from left to right and top to bottom, replace the original Chinese characters, which were arranged from top to bottom and right to left.

There were over seventy gambling operations in San Francisco Chinatown in the 1880s, most of them located in alleys and patronized by more than just Chinese players. Gambling was so popular in the West that local authorities simply could not stop it. Weekly bribes to local police ensured its smooth operation.[35] The immense interest in gambling was indicative of the social realities of the American West. Workers were attracted to the West by its promise of work and an improvement in their impoverished lot. This economic incentive was perhaps also the driving force behind the popularity of gambling. In a game of chance a person's lot could quickly change, and large sums of money, otherwise unattainable, might be won with no effort.

In sum, the so-called vices and low life of Chinatown,

34. Introduction to the reprint of Culin's work; no page number [p. 1].
35. Liu Boji, *History*, p. 120.

often cited by anti-Chinese elements to justify Chinese
exclusion, were part and parcel of the nineteenth-
century American West. Prostitution and gambling
were everywhere. Opium to the Chinese was like al-
cohol to the white men. In fact, alcohol created just as
many social problems in the white community as opium
did in the Chinese one, if not more.[36] Therefore, most
of the criticism was actually racially motivated. The
prevalence of these problems in San Francisco was also
due to corruption within the government: the author-
ities allowed the import and sale of opium until addic-
tion became more than a Chinese problem; and, by
accepting bribes from the operators of Chinatown
brothels, opium dens, and gambling houses, they al-
lowed these vices to continue without interference. The
true victims were, of course, the participants who ven-
tured into such an existence in search of a moment of
solace, a dream of wealth, or simply an escape from
reality.

CHINATOWN HIGH LIFE:
A LITERARY PRIDE

The literary legacy of San Francisco's Chinese Amer-
icans is not widely known because in studying the past
the major focus has always been on the labor aspects of

36. When Ng Poon Chew, a well-respected Chinese Christian
and publisher of the well-regarded San Francisco Chinese daily, the
Chung Sai Yat Po, was confronted with the issue of Chinese opium
addiction, he supported the call to eradicate opium but rejected the
anti-Chinese rhetoric behind it. Likening the ills of opium addiction
to alcoholism, which was prevalent in white society, he stated that
opium weakened the user, disarming him from dangering anyone
else, whereas alcohol made the drinker a dangerous person whose
unruly behavior would harm others. He joked that a wife could
beat her opium-addicted husband, but she would be beaten by her
alcoholic husband.

post-1860s Chinese immigration. Because of subsequent years of segregation, however, Chinese Americans also became second-class citizens in the English language. The population of school-age Chinese American children grew from about five hundred in 1867 to four thousand in 1900, with at least 75 percent of them residing in San Francisco.[37] However, until the 1930s, hardly any of them excelled at creative expression in the English language. This area of intellectual endeavor remained beyond their reach. Chinese Americans gained English-language skills first through missionary programs in Chinatown and later in segregated public schools.[38] But fluency in English was not enough to enable them to break into the white man's white-collar society. A Chinese American who was fluent in both English and Chinese might use this language ability to become a *cheut faan* (*chu fan*, lit. "out to the barbarians"), a kind of translator-representative hired by Chinese organizations to negotiate with the white men. At best, he might be employed as the official *chyun wa* (*chuan hua*, interpreter) for court or immigration cases involving non–English-speaking Chinese. Thus, early Chinatown residents could demonstrate practical English skills, but not literary ones.

However, this was not the case insofar as Chinese-language skills were concerned. Rampant racial preju-

37. Coolidge, p. 436.
38. For an extensive study of the history and issues of education confronting the Chinese in San Francisco, see Victor Low, *The Unimpressible Race: A Century of Educational Struggle by the Chinese in San Francisco* (San Francisco: East/West, 1982). Chinese Americans have consistently challenged racial segregation. However, in 1906, a public school located north of Stockton Street, between Clay and Washington streets, was established for "Oriental" students. Only the Japanese were able to successfully challenge segregated schools.

dice had early on convinced most Chinatown residents of the merchant class that the future of the younger generation would be in China, because they would never be accepted in America. Thus, many parents made special efforts to equip their offspring with Chinese skills in preparation for their future in China. There were over a dozen private Chinese tutorial schools in Chinatown in the 1870s,[39] and in 1888 a community-supported Chinese-language school was established. Students were taught from the traditional Chinese texts—classics, belles lettres, and historical writings. Also, many youngsters were sent back to China to receive a Chinese education, a practice akin to that of San Francisco high-society families who sent their children to the East Coast for a "proper" education. Many American-born Chinese excelled in their Chinese studies; some were even able to pass through the imperial examination system. For instance, an American-born Chinese named Jeung Siucheung (Zhang Shaoxiang), a graduate of the Chinatown Chinese-language school, sent back to South China for further studies at the age of fourteen, later passed the regional level of the imperial examination (i.e., *xiang shi*) and obtained the prestigious *xiucai* degree in 1904.[40]

Thus, there was no shortage of cultural expression among the immigrant generation in San Francisco

39. Him Mark Lai, "Meiguo Huaqiao jian shi" (A brief history of the Overseas Chinese in America), 38th installment of a serialized column in San Francisco's *Shidai Bao* (December 24, 1980), p. 2.

40. Liu Boji, *History*, pp. 356–57. The Chinese imperial examination system had three major testing levels; each consisted of a battery of examinations to test the candidates' writing skills. The first (base) exam was conducted on the local/regional level; successful candidates would be conferred the *xiucai* ("talented man")

Chinatown. In fact, their literacy level must have been quite high, since the first community newspaper began to circulate in 1854[41] and several more papers appeared in later years. In 1900, the *Chung Sai Yat Po* was established by Ng Poon Chew, a Christian. It became an influential daily in the Chinatown communities. In 1908, it instituted a daily supplement that frequently printed historical writings, prose, fiction, poetry, and popular Cantonese vernacular rhymes and satires. Then in 1909 the *Sai Gai Yat Po* also came into existence. Its editor, C. K. Leang (Liang Chaojie), was a leader of the Chinatown literati community. The two dailies frequently advertised books and other writings from San Francisco Chinatown's ten bookstores. Tai Quong, Fat Ming, and Sun Tai Lok were the best-known booksellers and publishers, and carried numerous dictionaries, English-language primers, and books on accounting, health and hygiene, current Chinese and world affairs, and geography. They also sold works of popular Can-

degree. The intermediate examination was conducted on the provincial level, usually in the provincial capital; successful candidates would receive the *juren* ("outstanding man") degree. The highest level, the "palace examination," was held in the imperial capital, and successful candidates would receive the *jinshi* ("advanced scholar") degree, with the top three candidates receiving special designations. The examinations were held once every three years, with special ones held on exceptional occasions as decreed by the emperor. The imperial examination system was the only ladder to success for men of letters who desired to hold government office. This system was abolished in 1905. For an extensive study of the system, see Deng Siyu, *Zhongguo kaoshi zhidu shi* (A history of the Chinese examination system) (Taibei: Xuesheng shudian, 1966).

41. Karl Lo and Him Mark Lai, "Introduction," in *Chinese Newspapers Published in North America, 1854–1975* (Washington, D.C.: Center for Chinese Research Materials, Association of Research Libraries, 1977), p. 2.

tonese literature as well as traditional Chinese classics
and histories. Hence, Chinatown's population was able
to sustain a market for books ranging from popular to
highbrow.

In addition, the leaders of the organizations under the
umbrella of the Six Companies were men of letters of
their respective districts who held at least the *xiucai*
degree. They were appointed by the district organiza-
tions in San Francisco as district presidents or chairmen
for a tenure of a specific number of years before return-
ing to China. The president of the Six Companies was
appointed in a similar fashion. Therefore, there was
always a group of Cantonese literati in the San Francisco
Chinese community. They often held gatherings known
as the *nga jaap* (*ya ji* "refined meeting," a euphemistic
expression for a gathering of poets taken from the *Book
of Songs* [*Shi jing*]). At each meeting a topic would be
suggested and members would write poems on that
subject. Poems and parallel couplets (*duilian*) were the
most popular form of creative expression among China-
town literati. Huang Zunxian, a Cantonese and well-
known Chinese poet in the late Qing period who was
consul general in San Francisco from 1881 to 1885,
actively organized and encouraged them, holding fre-
quent gatherings to inspire their writings. A poetry soci-
ety was formed.[42] Men of letters from Victoria, British
Columbia, another major Chinese settlement in the
West, later joined Huang's well-publicized group and
participated in the literary exchanges among group
members.

42. Liu Boji, *Meiguo Huaqiao shi xu bian* (English title: *A History
of the Chinese in the United States of America, II*) (Taibei: Liming
wenhua shiye gongsi, 1981), p. 404. (Hereafter cited as *History II*.)

In the spring of 1886, another literary society, the Xiao Peng Shi She (Paradise Poetry Club), was founded in Chinatown. In May that year, its members wrote over one hundred poems and presented them to Zhang Yinhuan, the envoy of China to the United States, gracefully asking for Zhang's comments and evaluations.[43] This practice of submitting one's writings to officials of higher rank was a common practice in imperial China, serving as a form of self-introduction in the process of seeking recognition and acceptance.

Other literary societies such as the Tong Wen She (Associates of Letters) and the Wen Hua She (Literary Splendor Society) were well established years before the 1906 earthquake and had numerous members. In 1888, the Tong Wen group also sent out their poetic couplets to Zhang Yinhuan when he toured Peru on behalf of the imperial government. This group's reputation for couplet-writing activities reached far beyond the Chinese communities in the San Francisco Bay area. When the group, to celebrate the Spring Festival of 1911, sponsored a couplet-writing competition, contestants from as far away as Canada, Peru, Mexico, and Cuba sent in compositions. Thus, there was a well-organized and established literary network among the Chinese on the American continent.

The Wen Hua Club was even more influential and active on the local level. It had over one hundred and fifty dues-paying members and a clubhouse at Brenham Place (recently changed to Walter Lum Place), opposite Portsmouth Plaza, where a shrine to Wen Chang, the patron god of letters, was installed. Incense was burned

43. Liu Boji, *History II*, p. 404.

and offerings were attended to daily, and celebrations marked festive occasions throughout the year. The society strictly observed the Confucian emphasis on and respect for writing, to the point of showing reverence for all writings. Hence it employed a "paper collector," who, carrying a club-issued gray cloth sack, would patrol the streets of Chinatown from early morning until late afternoon, picking up all discarded paper on the streets and collecting it from the stores.[44] He would then take the paper back to the clubhouse, where it would be burned. To show the club's respect for the privacy of others, no one ever looked at the contents. An incinerator was built in the shrine for this ritual burning. The ashes were placed in the gray sack, and, once a week, the club would hire a horse and wagon to take them to the pier; a boat would then ferry them out to the Golden Gate and empty them into the ocean. This elaborate ceremony for "paper garbage" was the club's demonstration of its utmost respect for writing, showing themselves as true disciples of the Confucian teaching that writing was the constitution of literacy. However, the non-Chinese looked upon this extremely dignified activity as only one more baffling example of Chinatown's exotic behavior, one among the many curious and eccentric practices of Chinatown.[45] Without understanding the Confucian motive behind the action, they saw it as merely "strange," and the ritual served to perpetuate the stereotype of the Chinese as an "unimpressible race."

The Wen Hua clubhouse was destroyed in the 1906

44. Tchen, p. 52, plate 52.
45. McLeod, pp. 256–69.

disaster, and the paper collection was discontinued shortly thereafter. However, the group continued its literary activities in the post-1906 years, as, rather amazingly, did most of the other literary groups. Shortly after the quake and fire, announcements of literary activities were to be found alongside those of community organizations and district groups rebuilding their destroyed Chinatown, especially in the *Chung Sai Yat Po*. Between 1906 and 1909, over a dozen literary groups announced activities, for the most part poetry and couplet writing contests. Some groups established temporary headquarters across the bay in Oakland. This feast of literary activities was quite unusual, given the destruction and chaos of the time, and, later, the community emphasis on economic reconstruction. But it demonstrated the unbroken existence of literary life in Chinatown at a time when the common perception of Chinatown in many non-Chinese writings dwelled on its "low life."

The early 1900s was a period of continuous growth for literary Chinatown, aided by the presence of many prominent and progressive men of letters such as Kang Youwei and Liang Qichao, who fled China after the reform movement failed in 1898. Although Kang never went to San Francisco, only to Victoria and Los Angeles, his followers nevertheless established a strong base in San Francisco Chinatown. In 1909, Kang's political party, the Bao Huang Dang (Royalist Party, later renamed the Xianzheng Dang, "Constitutional Party"), started the Chinatown daily *Sai Gai Yat Po*. Its editor, the scholar C. K. Leang, was a leader in literary activities, as we have seen, and through the *Sai Gai Yat Po* press, he also published many of his own writings.[46] In subsequent years, community literary activities expanded to writing competitions in various genres, including classical poetry, prose, and political essays. Their topics ranged from leisure-class interests ("A Warm Night by the Lotus Pond") to contemporary ones ("Riding an Airplane over the Rockies") to political and social ones ("On China's National Affairs"), with each competition attracting over a hundred contestants.[47] In July 1915, the topic of a poetry competition sponsored by the Hua Zhi Club was "Hardships of the Chinese Overseas," a subject dear to their own experience in the United States.

The many literary contests were publicly announced and entries were judged by well-respected scholars in the community. Top winners were usually awarded cash prizes and citations, and some of the works were anthologized and published.[48] Literary life in Chinatown continued to be active in the 1920s, when another influential poetry society, the Jinmen Yin She (Golden Gate Poetry Club), was formed by literati from the Seiyup and Saamyup districts. The society published an anthology of poetry in San Francisco in 1924.[49]

During the late 1910s and early 1920s, an unpre-

46. C. K. Leang, under the pen name of Chuyun Guan Juren, published many books, including two collections of essays both entitled *Chuyun Guan wen ji* (1922, 1926) and poetry collections that included *You Mei si ci cun gao* (1930), *Liang shi xiao ya* (1934), and *Wu guang shi se* (1941).

47. Liu Boji, *History II*, p. 406.

48. For example, a collection from the Caoxiang Group entitled *Cao xiang ya ji* (A collection of poems by the Caoxiang Club) (San Francisco: Nanhua shuju, 1934).

49. Jinmen Yin She, ed., *Jinmen Yin She shi ji* (A collection of poems by the Golden Gate Poetry Club) (San Francisco: Fat Ming Company, 1924).

cedented literary reform movement, later called the
May Fourth literary movement, was launched in China.
Many of its advocates were American-trained. They
called for a reform in the Chinese written language,
replacing classical Chinese with vernacular language.[50]
However, this "New Literature" movement appar-
ently had no effect on the Chinatown literary climate
at the time, despite the strong emphasis of the China-
town literati on cultural and ethnic identification with
China during the period of rejection in the United
States. Chinatown's indifference to the cultural re-
form is even more interesting if one considers the fact
that the reform was first advocated by writers like Hu
Shi, who had studied in the United States and whose
philosophy for reform was basically American-based.
The failure of literary reform in China to make an im-
pression on Chinatown's literary community can per-
haps be best explained by the fact that Chinatown's
resident literati were mostly traditionally educated Can-
tonese. They had little if any social interaction with the
Chinese reformers, who were non-Cantonese. Earlier
political reformers such as Kang Youwei, Liang Qichao,
and Sun Yatsen were Cantonese and had come to
America to solicit support and build a power base in the
Chinatown community. However, although cultural
reformers like Hu Shi had studied for many years in the
United States, they had never made an effort to become
active in the Chinatown community.[51] In fact, Hu's

50. For an excellent study of this movement, see Tse-tsung
Chow, *The May Fourth Movement: Intellectual Revolution In Modern
China* (Cambridge: Harvard University Press, 1960).
51. Perhaps one notable exception was Wen Yiduo (1899–
1946). When Wen was studying art in New York as a student in

advocacy of the modernization of China's literary tradition was based on the idea of a "wholesale Westernization" of China, something most unlikely to be accepted in Chinatown, as the community jealously safeguarded its Chinese tradition and cultural heritage. Its literati were intent on maintaining a sense of belonging, dignity, and purpose in an America whose political system and social practices had denied Chinese the right to participate in national life. Hence, literary Chinatown remained basically conservative, unaffected by the literary reform, and holding on to traditional literary expression. The situation did not change until the 1930s, when the Sino-Japanese War and the rise of Marxist ideology in China became forces that brought about a new literary era in Chinatown.[52]

Cantonese Folk Literature about the American Experience

THE AMERICAN SOJOURN
AS SEEN FROM GUANGDONG

The massive emigration of Cantonese natives to the United States beginning with the Gold Rush days had a tremendous effect on the social and economic condi-

---

1924–25, he wrote a poem entitled "Xi yi qu" (Laundry song) about a Chinese laundryman. Wen used the hardship of the laundryman to illustrate his displeasure that this kind of life was humiliating for the dignified Chinese race. "Xi yi qu," first published in 1925, was later included in Wen's *Si shui* (Dead water) (Shanghai: Xinyue shudian, 1928).

52. For a brief reference to the literary development in Chinatown, see "Chinatown Literature during the Last Ten Years (1939–1949) by Wenquan," translated by Marlon K. Hom with an introduction, *Amerasia Journal* 9, no. 2 (1982): 75–100.

tions of the Guangdong region. Not only were the people's livelihood and education markedly improved with the inflow of remittances and other means of support from outside, but the emigrant experience also affected the literature of the region. The emigration created a new content for its oral literature of folk songs and other popular narrative rhymes. These works of folk literature were commonly known as *Gamsaan go* (*Jinshan ge*, or "Gold Mountain songs"), and their content dealt primarily with the effects of the natives' emigration to America. For example, one popular song told, in hyperbole, of a Cantonese native's sojourn in the United States in 1852:

咸豐二年造金山，
担起遙仙萬分難 ；
竹篙船，
撐過海，
離婦別姐去求財 ；
唔掛房中人女，
唔掛二高堂 。

In the second reign year of Haamfung, a trip
    to Gold Mountain was made.
With a pillow on my shoulder, I began my perilous
    journey:
Sailing a boat with bamboo poles across the seas,
Leaving behind wife and sisters in search of money,
No longer lingering with the woman in the bedroom,
No longer paying respect to parents at home.[53]

53. Anon. (Tan Bi'an), "Jinshan fu xing" (Songs of the wife of a Gold Mountain man), *Xinning zazhi* 1100 (January 1949): 68. The second reign year of Haamfung (Xianfeng) of the Qing dynasty was 1852.

A song expressing the sojourner's sentiment from a participant's perspective was, however, a rarity. Most of the songs that circulated among the immigrants' homes focused on those who remained at home while husband, father, or relatives went to the United States. In 1929, Sun Yatsen University in Canton (Guangzhou), in a concerted effort to promote folklore studies advocated by the Academia Sinica in Peking, published an anthology of folk songs from Toisaan (Taishan),[54] whose natives constituted the largest Chinese group in America. Of the 203 locally collected folk songs, many deal with going overseas. Most of these are explicitly about the American journey; of these, some are children's ditties and some, songs of wives left behind. They have two basic themes: the expectation or promise of wealth from America and the wives' inevitable sorrow of separation.

The journey to America was regarded as an economic necessity, an opportunity for a man to secure a bright financial future for his family:

燕鵲喜，
賀新年；
爹爹去金山賺錢，
賺得金銀成萬兩，
返來起屋兼買田。

54. Chen Yuanzhu, ed., *Taishan geyao ji* (A collection of Taishan folk songs) (1929; rpt. Taibei: Folklore Books, 1969). There is also another collection of Cantonese folk songs available: Hu Zhaozhong, ed., *Meizhou Guangdong Huaqiao liuchuan geyao hui bian* (A collection of folk songs popular among the Cantonese in America) (Hong Kong: Zhendan tushu gongsi, 1970). Most of the 250 entries in Hu's collection can also be found in Chen's 1929 publication. Its claim that these folk songs were popular among the Cantonese in America has never been verified, though Chen's book shows that some of the songs were indeed concerned with the Gold Mountain journey from a non-participant perspective.

Swallows and magpies, flying in glee:
    Greetings for New Year.
Daddy has gone to Gold Mountain
    To earn money.
He will earn gold and silver,
    Ten thousand taels.
When he returns,
    We will buy a lot of land.[55]

爸爸去金山，
快快要寄銀，
全家靠住你，
有銀好寄回。

Father has gone to Gold Mountain.
Hurry up, send money home:
The whole family is depending on you;
When you get money, send it back, Hurry![56]

The economic incentive for going to the United States is further seen in another song, in which a journey to America is preferred to a journey anywhere else:

金山客，
冇一千有八百；
南洋客，
銀袋包，
大伯大伯；
香港仔，
香港賺錢香港使。

O, sojourner returning from Gold Mountain:
If you don't have one thousand dollars,
    You must have at least eight hundred.

55. Chen, song 87, p. 104.
56. Chen, song 127, p. 146.

O, uncle returning from the South Seas:
Just look at your money bag,
It's empty; it's all empty!

O, young man returning from Hong Kong:
You have earned money in Hong Kong
And spent it all in Hong Kong, too![57]

With America held in such high regard, it naturally followed that to marry "a man from Gold Mountain" was most desirable, far superior to marrying anyone else:

少小離鄉邦，
三十始回唐；
媒人來往走忙忙，
女母聞聲心中喜，
三句唔到就攬糖！

He left home at a young age, finally returning
to South China at thirty.
A matchmaker runs about in great haste.
A mother with a daughter hears about him,
joy fills her heart.
In less than three words, candy is accepted
as a proposal gift.[58]

有女莫嫁讀書君，
自己閂門自己睏；
有女莫嫁耕田人，
滿腳牛屎滿頭塵；
有女快嫁金山客，
一上船時銀成百。

57. Chen, song 59, p. 72.
58. Chen, song 38, pp. 49–50.

Don't marry a daughter to a man of books:
He locks himself behind doors and sleeps by himself.
Don't marry a daughter to a man who farms:
His feet covered with manure and his hair full of dust.
Hurry and marry the daughter to a man from Gold
   Mountain:
Once he gets off the boat, he has money all in hundred
   dollar bills.[59]

Other songs are expressions of the feelings of lonely
wives left behind in China while their husbands eked
out a living in America. On the surface, these women,
who were commonly known as *Gamsaanpo* (*Jinshan po*,
or "wives of Gold Mountain men") and were the envy
of those who lacked this American connection, lived on
handsome remittances, and led comparatively affluent
and comfortable lives. On the emotional level, how-
ever, due to the customary practice of wives staying
home while the men worked abroad,[60] the Gamsaanpo
suffered greatly, enduring a long and agonizing separa-
tion from their spouses, who sometimes vanished in
America without a trace. One common practice was for

59. Chen, song 1, p. 1.
60. As briefly mentioned earlier in the text, most Chinese men
were married before they came to the United States. It was custom-
ary for a Cantonese family to ensure that before leaving home the
man was married, in order to establish in him a sense of responsibility
and obligation to support the family. Another reason why wives
were left behind is that early Chinese emigration to the United
States was a labor movement. The conditions in America were not
suitable for many of them to establish permanent homesteads in
America, as was the case for most European immigrants during the
same period. American laws also disallowed Asian women from
coming. In 1924, the United States implemented exclusionary laws
specifically barring the entry of Asian women.

a marriage by proxy to be arranged for a young woman to a man who was still in America. The young bride would go through the entire wedding ceremony, but the marriage would not be consummated until the man returned.[61] Given this peculiar form of involuntary widowhood, it is not surprising that Seiyup folk songs about Gamsaanpo are full of complaint and grievance:

> 我君貧窮到金山，
> 本錢細小未得返；
> 想起金山條路十分艱難，
> 家裏淒涼望穿眼；
> 不及在家耕田好，
> 半年辛苦，半年閒，
> 朝見父母晚見妻子，
> 齊齊歡喜笑連連，
> 節節客客年卅晚，
> 夫男妻女幾風繁。

> My husband, pressed by poverty, took off
>   to Gold Mountain.
> With a petty sum of money, he cannot make
>   the journey home.
> The road to Gold Mountain is extremely
>   perilous and difficult;
> At home, in grief and pain, my longing eyes
>   pierce through to the horizon, waiting for
>   his return.

61. In this proxy marriage practice, a rooster was used to represent the sojourning groom. The bride would go through the entire wedding ceremony with the rooster by her side as her husband-to-be. This practice was common among the Cantonese in the Pearl River delta and has been described in many creative writings. See "Jinshan fu xing" (n. 53 above) for an example.

O, no way is such a life better than that of
    farming at home:
Toiling for half a year, relaxing the rest;
You greet parents in the morning;
You are with your wife at night;
Everyone is happy, with smiles all over their
    faces;
Festivals, parties, New Year's Eve celebrations—
You and I, husband and wife, O, how loving
    would that be![62]

別鄉井，
出外洋，
十年八載不思鄉；
柳色毿毿陌頭綠，
閨中少婦惱斷腸。

You bid farewell to the village well, setting out for
    overseas.
It's been eight years, or is it already ten, and
    you haven't thought of home.
Willow branches are now brilliant, fields exuberantly
    green;
In her bedroom, the young woman's bosom is filled
    with frustration and grief.[63]

青春守生寨，
枕冷令人怕；
想來想去亂如麻，
千里遙遙難共話；
細想他，
輾轉猶然也；

62. "Jinshan fu xing," p. 68.
63. Chen, song 37, p. 49.

雖在天邊雲腳下，
三更尤望佢回家。

I am still young, with a husband, yet I'm a widow.
The pillow is cold, frighteningly cold.
Thoughts whirl in my mind, as chaotic as hemp
  fibers.
Separated by thousands of miles, how can I
  reach him?
Thinking of him tenderly—
I toss and turn, to no avail.
He's far away, at the edge of the sky by the
  clouds.
At midnight, I long all the more for his return
  now.[64]

Given the misery and frustration of such an existence
it should come as no surprise that, despite its promise of
a comfortable life, such a marriage is held up to question-
ing in several folk songs:

有女儘嫁金山佬，
金山箱仔任你敊；
有女莫嫁金山佬，
丟奴冷薄熬砂煲。

O, just marry all the daughters to men from
  Gold Mountain:
All those trunks from Gold Mountain—
    You can demand as many as you want!
O, don't ever marry your daughter to a man
  from Gold Mountain:
Lonely and sad—
    A cooking pot is her only companion![65]

64. Chen, song 201, p. 238.
65. "Jinshan fu xing," p. 69.

有女勿嫁讀書君，
自己關門自己睏；
有女勿嫁耕田人，
滿身泥氣鬱死人；
有女勿嫁金山客，
別個家庭唔記得；
有女盡嫁生意仔，
朝魚晚肉好心才。

Don't marry a daughter to a man of books:
He locks himself up behind doors and sleeps by
    himself.
Don't marry a daughter to a man who farms:
His body is filled with the smell of mud and will
    suffocate her to death.
Don't marry a daughter to a man from Gold Mountain:
Once he leaves home, home he will forget.
It's best to marry a daughter to a young merchant:
With fish for lunch and meat for supper, he's the
    most considerate.[66]

Other Cantonese vernacular genres also adopted Gold
Mountain themes in their depiction of the life of the
sojourner. In the genre of rhythmic chants known as the
muk yu go (*mu yu ge*, or "wood-fish songs"),[67] there are

66. Chen, song 89, p. 106.
67. *Muk yu go* is a Cantonese vernacular rhymed narrative.
There are two theories as to its origin. One claims that it comes
from the folk songs of the Cantonese boat people living along the
Pearl River and its tributaries. The other theory is that it is bor-
rowed from the Buddhist practice of chanting sutras to the beating
of a red wooden block, shaped like a fish head. The rhythmic
chanting tells a story. These narratives have been published, mostly
in Canton and Hong Kong, for readers to use as a chant-along. This
genre of vernacular oral/written story-telling is popular among
both Cantonese peasants and the merchant class, and its wide circu-
lation in San Francisco Chinatown is indicated by book advertise-

a few extant pieces on the Gamsaanpo's life that were also in circulation in America's Chinatown. One piece, entitled "Laments of the Wife of a Gold Mountain Man" ("Jinshan po zi tan"),[68] is a first-person narrative of a young wife waiting anxiously for her husband to return. The chant manipulates monthly calendar events and seasonal festivals to emphasize the wife's state of separation-induced loneliness and grief. On each occasion, the gaiety of the outside world is juxtaposed against the wife's sadness. She perpetually wishes for her husband's return, a futile expectation that only fuels her despair and resentment upon the arrival of Chinese New Year, traditionally a time for family reunions:

> …
> 夫君你好回歸轉，
> 等你不歸眼望穿；
> 入到房中嘆大氣，
> 只估我君在床前；
> 雙手隨床摩到邊，
> 摩着衣裳照見面，
> 縱然命短死亦甜。
> …
> 待等明年還再望，
> 家家主主貼紅錢，
> 揮春大吉多興旺，
> 福祿壽三星貼在門前。
> 人家團圓夫妻樂，

---

ments. For a study of this genre, see Liang Pui-chee, *Wooden-Fish Books, Critical Essays and an Annotated Catalog Based on the Collection in the University of Hong Kong* (Hong Kong: University of Hong Kong, 1978).

68. Anon., "Jinshan po zi tan" (N.p.: Cang ji chubanshe, n.d.).

香花燭臘千萬千；
鳳鵝豬頭還多買，
竹炮燒响起塵烟；
自己團圓揸苦練，
蜜糖入口都不甜。
來世學花不做女，
叠埋心水練神仙。

. . .

Dear Husband, it's time to make the journey home.
My longing eyes pierce through the horizon.
You are nowhere in sight.
I return to the bedroom with heavy sighs.
>   In a flash I see you by the bed.
>   I hold myself by the bedside, with both hands
>   on the edge;
>   I try to touch your clothes; I want to feel
>   your face.
>   O, even if this means a shorter life, I won't
>   begrudge it!

. . .

So comes the New Year;
>   Still I must wait for you.
Red paper coins decorate houses everywhere;
New Year scrolls proclaim good fortunes.
Images of the Three Immortals of Happiness,
     Longevity, and Prosperity grace the front door.
All over the place, thousands of flowers are sweet and
     candles bright.
Families are together as husband and wife unite.
In abundance, chicken and pork are prepared;
Loud firecrackers burst off clouds of smoke.
And for me—
>   A time for reunion means a solitary retreat.
>   The taste of honey now is not at all sweet.

> O, I shall be wise and never reborn a girl again!
> I shall cultivate celibacy and the immortal deed![69]

In the genre of vernacular prose narrative, a tale entitled "Jit haau Waanwan" (Jie xiao huanhun) ("Chastity, filial piety, and reincarnation"),[70] written before the 1900s by a Cantonese writer named Tong Santin (Tang Xintian), tells the story of Chan Baakhong (Chen Bokang), a native of Sunwui (Xinhui, of the Seiyup), who goes on a journey to America to seek a living for his family. However, he is barely able to survive, let alone support his family. A laborer, he is stranded for nineteen years in the mines, unable to contact his family. His wife and mother live a meager existence while awaiting his return. Years pass and rumor has it that Chan has died in America. His mother is in poor health, and his wife, who is a filial daughter-in-law, pawns what is left of her belongings and clothing to prepare a good meal for her elderly mother-in-law, telling her falsely that Chan has finally struck it rich in America and is sending money to them. The old woman is overjoyed, but later, when she hears a rumor of her son's death, she dies in grief. After the mourning period, the people in the village suggest that Chan's wife remarry, but she steadfastly refuses and commits suicide instead.

Meanwhile, Chan still toils in America. One day,

69. "Jinshan po zi tan," p. 5.
70. The publication data for this story are unknown. It is the first entry in a collection entitled *Yong yan she qu* (Trivial but interesting words), vol. 2, pp. 1–12. It is written in colloquial Cantonese. There are two editions of this anthology. One has no publication data. The compilation of the other edition is attributed to Tang Yincai. It was published in Canton in 1896. Tang Yincai and Tang Xintian appear to be the same person.

luck finally comes to him when he claims a huge gold nugget in a mine. With that comes plenty of money, and he hurries home after his prolonged absence, only to find out what has happened. The story then moves into the supernatural realm, as Chan's wife returns to life in a surrogate body, and they are rewarded for their filial piety and for her chastity.

This story is significant in that Chan's journey to America is consistent with the economic aspects of the early Chinese labor immigration patterns. His hardship in America is only casually mentioned and not discussed in detail, probably due to the narrator's lack of personal experience. However, the American experience functions effectively as the catalyst for the story's development: the hardship endured by Chan in America is the cause of all the grief at home. In fact, the story is an indictment of the glorified journey that does not necessarily reward the participants with the promised wealth.

On another occasion, a Cantonese man of letters from the late Qing period (ca. 1880s) looks at the sorrow of a forsaken wife and poignantly states that it was a direct result of the economic hardship endured by her spouse in America:

> At first, there were indeed a couple [of emigrants] who returned with some profit. Subsequently, many flocked over there. Gradually the gold mines were exhausted. Many became displaced drifters in a foreign land and died there. Those who were able to survive numbered no more than one or two out of a hundred.
>
> When they first put up their fare for the journey [to Gold Mountain], they could do no better than borrow money from friends and relatives, or sell land and property. As their wishes were betrayed and they were

unable to save even enough money to return home, they simply showed no more concern for their parents, wives, and children.[71]

CANTONESE RHYMES FROM SAN FRANCISCO CHINATOWN

The experience of the Cantonese immigrants in the United States at the turn of the century has been vividly preserved in vernacular writings and folk songs. Numerous Cantonese popular writings had appeared in newspapers in Chinatown. Most of them were humorous pieces, poking fun at prostitutes, opium addicts, gamblers, and so forth. There were always folk songs and other vernacular writings published in the supplement to the *Chung Sai Yat Po*. The widespread popular acceptance of the genres among the Chinese American communities was probably due to the fact that creative expression in the Cantonese vernacular was widely accepted among the Cantonese men of letters living in Chinatown. They might write formal poetry (i.e., classical poetry) on serious or "refined" occasions, but they would also write vernacular pieces for entertainment on other less serious occasions.

Besides being published in Chinatown, some works found their way to publication in China, as a result of the close relationship between the "home" community and the Chinatown abroad. Many Cantonese vernacular pieces appeared in Canton during the 1905 national movement to boycott American goods in protest of the United States' unfair extension of Chinese exclusion laws. For example, there is a *muk yu* narrative entitled "Lamentation of a Gold Mountain Man at Night"

71. "Jinshan fu xing," p. 68.

("Jinshan ke tan wu geng"),[72] written anonymously in the first person about immigrant life in America. In addition to expressing economic concerns, the work keenly relates feelings of banishment and indignation over the agony and injustice of the American sojourn; none of these concerns is to be found in any other Cantonese folk song from China. The participant's perspective is also found in another piece of prose, entitled "Preface to Detention in the Wooden Barracks" ("Muwu juliu xu").[73] It was first published in the *Sai Gai Yat Po* (which deleted a few lines that were critical of the Manchu government). A year later, the complete version appeared in the *Xinning zazhi*,[74] a Toisaan publication that also enjoyed wide circulation in America. The prose work deals with the harsh and unequal treatment that the Chinese received in the American immigration station. This complete version also reveals a politically explicit and critical voice.

More significant in the development of early Chinatown literature was the publication in San Francisco of two anthologies of Chinatown folk rhymes. The first, entitled *Jinshan ge ji* (Songs of Gold Mountain) and consisting of 808 pieces, was published in 1911 by Tai Quong Company, a noted Chinatown bookseller and publisher. It cost one dollar. There was no exact count as to how many copies were printed and sold; however,

72. This piece is collected in A Ying, ed., *Fan Mei Hua gong yinyue wenxue ji* (A collection of literature opposing the American exclusion of Chinese laborers) (Beijing: Zhonghua shuju, 1960), pp. 677–78.

73. "Muwu juliu xu," *Sai Gai Yat Po* (January 16, 1910). For an English translation of this prose work, see *Island: Poetry and History of Chinese Immigrants on Angel Island*, comp. and trans. by Him Mark Lai et al. (San Francisco: Hoc Doi, 1980), pp. 138–41.

74. "Muwu juliu xu," *Xinning zazhi* 28 (1911): 76–78.

it quickly sold out. Popular demand led to publication in 1915 of an additional 832 rhymes under the title *Jinshan ge erji* (Songs of Gold Mountain, volume 2). These two volumes contain a total of 1,640 vernacular rhymes in the Cantonese folk song format known as *seisapluk ji go* (*sishiliu zi ge*, or "forty-six-syllable song"). They represent the largest collection of Cantonese folk rhyme writings ever published anywhere.

In their formal structure, these folk rhymes have forty-six syllables, which are arranged in an eight-line pattern of 5-5-7-7-3-5-7-7, with each line ending in a rhyming syllable, as illustrated in the following:[75]

Content							*Rhyme scheme*
守	家	多	失	策			
sau	ka	tɔː	sət	tɕ'aːk			[aːk]
百	謀	方	旅	墨			
paːk	mau	fɔːŋ	leu	mək			[ək]
政	黨	相	持	狼	虎	革	
tɕeŋ	tɔːŋ	sœːŋ	tɕ'iː	lɔːŋ	fu	kaːk	[aːk]
仇	視	外	人	財	命	索	
sau	si	ŋɔːi	yən	tɕ'ɔːi	mɛːŋ	sɔːk	[ɔːk]
唔	樓	得					
m	tɕ'aːi	tək					[ək]
偷	關	過	美	域			
t'au	kwaːn	kwɔː	mei	wɛk			[ɛk]
撞	着	稅	員	嚴	拉	冊	
tɕɔːŋ	tɕœːk	suːi	yuːn	yiːm	lai	tɕ'aːk	[aːk]
令	我	回	華	申	逐	客	
leŋ	ŋɔː	wuːi	wa	sən	tɕɔːk	haːk	[aːk]

75. *Jinshan ge erji* (San Francisco: Tai Quong Company, 1915), pp. 11a. This piece is translated as song 16 in this anthology. Hereafter, *Jinshan ge ji* (1911) and *Jinshan ge erji* (1915) will be abbreviated as JSGJ I and JSGJ II respectively.

Their structural arrangement appears to be rigid in comparison with the looser format of most other Cantonese folk songs. Most Cantonese folk songs have no specific convention as to the length or number of syllables, other than a rhyming scheme based on Cantonese phonology. On the surface, these forty-six-syllable songs share the rigid line pattern found in the genre of classical Chinese poetry known as the *ci*, which has flourished since the late Tang dynasty (ninth century): both the *ci* and the *seisapluk ji go* must have a specific number of syllables per line, and both have rhymed lines that are irregular in length but evenly matched. However, the similarity ends there. The *ci*-poems and certain other classical Chinese poems also have an extremely regulated pattern of tonal metering for each syllable, commonly known as "tonal balance" (*pingze*),[76] but this is not a requirement of the forty-six-syllable song. Traditional Chinese poetics also require a rhyme scheme to stringently follow the conventions of the "rhyme books" (*yunshu*), in which the final of each syllable belongs to a given phonological or rhyming category and only syllables sharing the same classification can be used to form an acceptable rhyme scheme. The forty-six-syllable song does not adhere to this formal rhyming convention. As we saw in the example above, the rhyming scheme is rather loose; finals [aːk], [ək], [ɔːk], and [ɛk] are all regarded as rhyming since they are phonetically similar in Cantonese.

It has been claimed that these Chinatown folk rhymes

76. For a detailed study of Chinese poetics, particularly of the formal structure of the different poetic forms in classical Chinese poetry, see Wang Li, *Hanyu shilü xue* (A study of Chinese poetics) (Shanghai: Shanghai jiaoyu chubanshe, 1962). See chapter 3, pp. 508–683, for a study on *ci* poetics.

have a unique format, different from, though somewhat
similar to, that of regular Cantonese folk songs.[77] How-
ever, folk songs with an identical format are also found
in Toisaan county.[78] Liang Shouping, author of the
brief preface to the 1911 anthology, plainly states that
forty-six-syllable songs are Cantonese vernacular rhymes
based on the phonology of spoken Cantonese that need
not follow the standard Chinese rhyming and metering
system. He adds that the major requirement is that their
language consist of local expressions and be colloquial
enough for women and children to understand and learn
from the song.[79] Therefore, it is clear that the forty-
six-syllable song format is a genuinely Cantonese folk
song pattern that differs only because it deals with the
American experience and is the product of San Francisco
Chinatown. The Chinatown writers merely utilized this
Cantonese pattern for their own creation.

In addition to the above-mentioned format, some
rhymes follow a "word game" format. Here, a theme
word, usually a noun or a verb, which is sometimes
used with another word to form a compound, is re-
quired on every line. The repetition of the particular
word both defines the song's theme and illustrates the
writer's skill at arriving at a variety of expressions using
the same thematic word. For example, "dream" (*meng*)
or "hometown / village" (*xiang*) are frequently used in
songs dealing with nostalgic emotions; "wealth" (*cai*) or

77. Li Boji, *History II*, p. 407.
78. Cf. Chen Yuanzhu's 1929 collection of folk songs. Songs 124
and 201 are of the forty-six-syllable song format. Song 201 has been
translated in this introduction; see n. 64 above.
79. Liang Shouping, "Preface," in JSGJ I (San Francisco:
Tai Quong Company, 1911), pp. 1a–1b.

"money" (*qian*), dealing with the wish to become rich; "flower" (*hua*), dealing with women. The repetition of the theme word in such a short piece makes these rhymes either extremely emotionally laden or comically lighthearted. It was both a challenge and a game for the writers to be innovative under such rules.

Although these folk rhymes were called "playful inkings by celebrities" of San Francisco Chinatown,[80] sometimes they dealt with matters beyond San Francisco Chinatown in scope. Apparently, many were contributed by writers who lived or had lived as far away as Mexico or Canada. Individual authors, however, were not identified, in keeping with the traditional Chinese practice of maintaining anonymity in the publication of vernacular or vulgar literature, which was frowned on by Confucian teaching. Nevertheless, "teachers," that is, men of letters in the Chinatown community, were given credit as judges and reviewers of these rhymes. For the 1911 anthology, there were fifteen teachers, and for the 1915 one, fourteen. All well-known in Chinatown, they included leaders of the seven largest district associations, editors of newspapers, Chinese-language school teachers, and scholars.[81] This was a project that transcended Seiyup-Saamyup or any other district barriers, as men of letters from all regional backgrounds participated.

It is possible that these folk rhymes were the result of some collective writing activity in San Francisco Chinatown. A topic would be announced and a "teacher" put

80. This statement appears on the cover of the 1915 anthology, and the preface states that the writings come from San Francisco Chinatown.
81. Liu Boji, *History II*, pp. 407–8.

in charge of that topic. Writers would submit their compositions, which were in turn judged and selected by the teacher for publication. Some of the teachers did so for more than three topics. Within each category, some pieces share extremely similar content and language usage. However, the possibility that these rhymes could have been written by the same author seems remote. Rather than repeating his own expressions, it seems more likely that a writer would choose to display his broader creative talents within the same given topic. Similar pieces were written by different writers, perhaps as a result of their response to each other's inspiration and views on the same topic. The preface to the 1915 anthology states that it was the product of over thirty writing activities with over one hundred contributors.[82] Given that the Chinese population in San Francisco was less than fourteen thousand in the early 1910s, this indicates an enormous response from the community.

As mentioned earlier, the language used in the rhymes is colloquial Cantonese. It is folksy, somewhat vulgar, and at times erotic. Some of the pieces contain faultily written characters, either unintentional mistakes by writers or typographical errors. The errors reveal the unsophisticated peasant background of some of the writers, who became very uninhibited behind the mask of anonymity. The rhymes also contain many impromptu Chinese translations and transliterations of terms commonly used in the United States at the time. For example, terms such as "bicycle" [tɐi: / yau / tɵ′ɛ:], "emancipated woman" [tɐi: / yau / nɵü], "telephone" [ha:m / si:n], "yellow eagle" (a United States gold coin)

---

82. "Preface," JSGJ II, p. 1a.

[wɔːŋ / yeŋ], "Alpine" (a county in northeastern California, the Mother Lode) [aː / paːn], to name only a few, can be found in the two anthologies. Evidently coined by the Cantonese in America, these expressions were different from those used in China. Since some of the terms are no longer in vogue in today's Chinatown vocabulary, these folk rhymes provide an excellent glimpse of how early Chinese Americans improvised new expressions to accommodate and describe their American experience, thus developing their own unique language sensibility.

Numerous standard Chinese clichés and formulaic expressions can also be seen in these works. Many poetic images, allusions, and stock phrases are conventional, revealing little innovation from established usage. For example, "full moon" always alludes to a reunion, "clouds and rain" to sexual intimacy, "geese" to couriers of news, and so on. Hence, these writings may appear unoriginal and trite at first glance. Nevertheless, these "flaws" are evidence that the origin of the rhymes was from oral folk song, in which formulaic expressions and language usage are distinct features.

Most compilers of vernacular writings in old China emphasized that the function of the genre is to be didactic and to provide entertainment for the less educated. For centuries, even the folk songs in the Confucian classic *Shi jing*, China's first book of poetry, were studied for their didactic messages. The compilers of the two Chinatown folk rhyme anthologies shared the same traditional view of vernacular literature. In fact, the writer of the preface to the 1915 volume, under the guise of a pen name, even borrowed the views of Feng Menglong (?–1646), a famous compiler and writer of vernacular Chinese short stories of the late Ming period, to claim that vernacular writings serve the didactic function better than standard classics and historical writings do—the latter being uninspiring, while the former are more lively and entertaining. He even went a step further in regard to folk songs:

> When we study the *Record of History* or *History of the Han Dynasty*, we all get sleepy. But if we read the *West Chamber* or *Water Margin*, each of us would be full of interest and energy. The brisk and refreshing nature of a folk song is even more exquisite than the *West Chamber* or *Water Margin*. In it, every sound has rhythm. If sung in our local dialect, every word rhymes. If put into a tune, it is acceptable to both the refined and the vulgar. It is playful but not at all crude. It has both seriousness and humor. Its ideas are like a clear breeze, and its feelings, moving.[83]

As far as the content is concerned, there are thirty-four topic categories in the 1911 anthology, and thirty-three in the 1915 one. Many of the categories overlap in theme, as we can see from the chart on page 61.

Of the 1,640 original entries in the two anthologies, I have selected 220 pieces for this translation anthology. I have chosen them because I believe they best illustrate the life of the early Chinese Americans and Chinatown. From the original thirty-plus overlapping categories in each volume, I have grouped the pieces by theme into eleven categories.

Major themes deal with the immigrants' feelings of hardship and loneliness in America, their separation

83. Ibid., pp. 1a–1b.

Topics	Category/Chapter Number		Total
	1911 Anthology	*1915 Anthology*	
On immigration and related problems	3,* 10		1½
On hardship and poverty in America	4, 12	5, 6, 7, 8, 24, 32	8
On a wife's sorrow due to separation	14, 16, 31, 32, 33	19, 28	7
On homesickness and China	7, 9, 30, 34	21, 22, 23, 29, 30	9
On money and wealth	19, 27	2, 33	4
On Westernization and social conformity	6, 18	1, 9, 12, 16	6
On love and romance	17, 20, 21, 25, 29	18	6
On marriage and weddings	11, 15, 22, 23, 24, 26, 28	3, 20	9
On opium, gambling, and vices other than womanizing	1, 2, 5	4, 25, 26, 31	7
On womanizing	3,* 8	11, 14, 17	4½
On prostitutes	13	10, 13, 15, 27	5
Total	34	33	67

*Category no. 3 in the 1911 anthology is entitled *Meiren*, which can mean either "beautiful women" or "Americans." Its content covers trouble with both women and Americans.

from families, and their expreiences in the new land. The rhymes frequently express complaints of hardship and voice disappointment over the American sojourn. The economic motive for the Cantonese emigration to the United States was also pursuit of the American dream in the "land of opportunity." However, these Chinese immigrants soon realized that because of exclusionary practices in America and the white man's belief in manifest destiny, their status was that of unwelcome heathens and they were regarded as an inferior race. Instead of the opportunity to better themselves financially, their life often turned out to be a constant struggle for survival within a marginal existence. These folk rhymes poignantly reveal their disappointment at their failure to attain success and to fulfill their aspirations. Their disillusionment is explicit in the complaint that, even after laboring for scores of years in America, a country that prohibited their naturalization and denied them equal status, they were unable to get away and go home. The failure to realize their Gold Mountain Dream was both a wound to their egos and a betrayal of their mission in America.

The desire to return to China after attaining some kind of financial success is repeatedly expressed in many of these songs. This desire was often attacked during the exclusion days by anti-Chinese critics, who claimed that the Chinese could not assimilate into the greater American society since they were not here for permanent residency. However, critics failed to recognize a more objective explanation for the "sojourner's mentality" that was so pronounced among early Chinese immigrants. From the first, only males were recruited, and the immigration of their families was not encouraged. Second, most of these workers held transient jobs that were located outside a stable or urban environment, jobs such as mining or railroad construction that were not conducive to raising a family. Later, when under the exclusionary laws, Chinese immigrants were neither allowed to be naturalized nor permitted to own land. In California, interracial marriage for the Chinese was illegal. Thus, political and social policies did not provide favorable conditions for the Chinese to establish families and to stay permanently in America. Thus it was only natural that Chinese men would wish to return to China if they could. Hence, the sojourner's mentality was also a product of anti-Chinese practices.

Being a family man, away from home and unable to bring along his family, created tremendous hardships on the immigrant's mental well-being. The folk rhymes express the torment of separation from family extremely vividly, with the voice of frustration never understated. However, the pieces on separation contain an interesting phenomenon, which may seem peculiar to modern readers unfamiliar with traditional Asian culture: few of the rhymes deal specifically with a man's affection for his wife. Instead, most of them contain no direct male expression of conjugal sentiment, unless in the context of expressing affection for the man's parents, siblings, or children. But there are numerous rhymes written from the perspective of a wife, revealing her feelings and affection for the sojourning husband in America. Similar to the Toisaan folk songs in China, these rhymes express sympathy for the plight of the forsaken wives. In particular, they condemn the unbearable absence of physical affection, which they regard as a miserable, pitiful waste of the prime years of a woman's life.

Given the internal evidence in these rhymes, which contain impromptu transliterations of English terms, it is unlikely that they were written by women living in Toisaan. And given the social morality and sex ratio of the Chinatown population during the early 1900s, it is inconceivable that so many Chinese women would have been permitted to mingle actively in male-oriented literary circles. Nor is it likely that they would have written so frankly and intimately, as if they were back in China writing for their men to come home. No other aspect of their own life in America is mentioned. Therefore, it seems reasonable to conclude that these rhymes were in fact the creation of men living in America, men who took on female personae in their poetic expression of conjugal affection. In many of the poetic works of old China, men write in a feminine voice, particularly on the subject of conjugal affection or marital intimacy. Since the Cantonese men in America were also inhibited from directly expressing conjugal affection for their spouses, they likely also preferred to project themselves as wives expressing such feelings, as if the expression of conjugal affection were not masculine but the privilege of women.

By using the guise of a feminine persona, these men obviously emphasized the common belief that conjugal affection was an exclusively feminine emotion. They wrote what they believed their wives should feel during the separation, inevitably putting the husband at the center of the wife's existence. On the other hand, they also showed a keen understanding of the plight of their women. Their rhymes are comparable to the folk songs sung among Toisaan women. Therefore, to a certain extent, the Cantonese men in America were able to place themselves in their spouses' position and vehemently acknowledge what the American journey had done to their marital relationships. The agony of separation was a shared sorrow for both husband and wife.

Another substantial number of folk rhymes deal with the subjects of women, prostitutes, and sex, reflecting the strong desire for female companionship among the men in predominantly male Chinatown. We have seen earlier how the lopsided sex ratio created many social problems, such as prostitution. The population imbalance grew even more acute and permanent as laws were enacted to prohibit the entry of Asian women to America. Therefore, behind some of the rather farcical expressions of sexual fantasy in these folk writings, there existed an extremely troubling social phenomenon.

The attitude toward women that these rhymes express is somewhat paradoxical. Empathy is shown for the lonely wives. For the unfortunate women trapped in prostitution, there are remonstrations to leave the shameful profession. The women's suffrage movement in the United States and the emancipation of women are praised as bringing the status of women into the modern era of equality. However, there are numerous rhymes that treat women as objects for the fulfillment for men's sexual fantasy and gratification. For instance, in the rhymes on marriage and weddings, the primary depiction is physical, that is, sexual pleasure. In other rhymes, an old man's fornication with younger women serves to illustrate his vitality and youthfulness at heart. Furthermore, any Chinese woman who was Westernized, that is, whose behavior deviated from traditional Chinese practices, is denounced as licentious, cheap, and immoral.

Such contrasting attitudes about women are not particularly contradictory if we consider the conditions under which the Cantonese man lived in America. His depictions of women were based purely on his own needs. Some immigrants were apparently impressed by the Western democratic idea of equality for women, while others were still bound by the Confucian way of thinking, in which woman played a subjugated role. Thus, while some rhymes show approval of the modern idea of equality for women in general, others complain of Chinese women's becoming modernized. In addition, since these men lived in a community whose population was predominantly male, out of sheer physical need, they made women the objects of much interest, desire, and fantasy. Thus, while some men were sympathetic toward the plight of prostitutes and critical of prostitution, many nevertheless showed immense indulgence toward and a willing patronage of prostitutes.

Fantasy and desire extended beyond the depiction of women, however. Led by hardship to a desperate desire for wealth, they saw wealth as the absolute gauge of their success in America. It was in the tradition of the work ethic to believe also that frugality and endurance would eventually be rewarded with wealth and success. However, many of these immigrants knew that in reality their only hope of quickly becoming wealthy, or of having enough to finance a triumphant journey home, would be from a sudden opportunity to strike it rich in the States. Thus, they dreamed of unexpected gain: hitting a gold claim or finding some hidden treasure. Although gambling was considered a major vice, in their fantasy of wealth these men came to believe that gambling might provide a source of hope for them: through a game of chance, they could at least try their luck at materializing the Gold Mountain Dream. Rhymes on this theme reflect the desperation and fantastic thinking of the betrayed Chinese immigrants as they wishfully tried to seek solace in gambling.

There are also rhymes about the American-born children of those lucky enough to have families in the

United States. Before the rediscovery of these writings, there were few extant pieces of creative writing that dealt with American-born children of the early days. While the Chinese community was generally perceived as a "bachelor society," that is, predominantly male and transient, these rhymes reveal that Chinese American family units were already well established, mostly among the merchant class. With an increase from five hundred school-age Chinese children in the 1860s to about four thousand in the early 1900s, most of them in San Francisco, a new generation of Chinatown residents was born, whose behavior and lifestyle were often not at all similar to those of their immigrant parents.

It is significant that these few folk rhymes on the younger generation acknowledge the "non-Chinese" behavior of the new Chinatown generation, who were physically Chinese but Westernized in thought. This is an important recognition of their new cultural characteristics. However, the immigrant writers of these rhymes interpret the difference negatively. We have seen that in some rhymes the immigrants praise American culture as modern, liberal, and symbolizing progress and independence. However, the "Americanness" exhibited in American-born children was a disgrace to the immigrants' time-honored Confucian tradition, especially when American-born women refused to play a submissive role. They were regarded as wild and undisciplined, badly influenced by the "barbaric" Western culture. Some American-born women were even labeled women of ill repute and treated despicably, as if they had prostituted themselves. Unfortunately, this negative attitude toward the American-born generation is still evident among the immigrant generation today, the latter often calling American-borns *mou nou juk sing* ("brainless bamboo sections"), implying that they are ignorant and shallow, without any sign of intelligence.

Many rhymes reveal that the early immigrants did not live in sheltered alienation from the greater American society, but were influenced by the Western way of life and kept abreast of the important events of the American community. There are rhymes, for example, that comment on the women's suffrage movement. Some praise it as salvation for the many oppressed women; others, marked with chauvinistic contempt, offer sarcastic comments about emancipated women who turn around to bully their husbands, thereby throwing domestic order into chaos and destroying family peace of mind. These expressions, while of course playful, still show the state of mind of the Chinatown residents in that period. Most of the rhymes are didactic and rigidly prescribe to Confucian moral values. Gambling, opium addiction, womanizing, and the other vices of a bachelor society are sternly criticized, although gambling and womanizing are sometimes depicted as enjoyable and a needed indulgence for desperate men.

The viewpoint of a few of the rhymes, however, indicates a departure from the Confucian praise for the selfless individual who would conform and sacrifice himself for his family or for society. They express the view that one's own needs must take precedence over everything else. For instance, in the Confucian framework, having a son has always been regarded as an ethical obligation. A son also provides for the parents' security and comfort in the order of Confucian filial piety. But this belief is ridiculed in some of the rhymes, which state that wealth, a personal gain, is preferable to a son. This attitude perhaps was a rationalization, de-emphasizing the importance of family piety in the "familyless" existence of the Chinatown residents. This readjustment, coupled with a lopsided criticism of American-born children, indicates that a number of the immigrants were more concerned with their own immediate well-being, and were hence turning their backs on Chinese family ethics and Confucian piety. Ironically, though, these very forces were the reason for their perilous expedition to America in the first place.

In conclusion, the vernacular writings from Chinatown vividly reflect the dynamic life of the early Chinese immigrants, most of whom came from a peasant or merchant background. The works are folksy, artistic illustrations of the early immigrants' experience in the United States; they are the aesthetic echoes and records of the immigrants' own sentiments. As a result, they offer an unusual perspective on early Chinatown life. As writers and readers of these works, the Cantonese immigrants might have also gained from them a sense of belonging and identification, seeing that their own personal experiences in America were actually shared by their fellow countrymen. The immigrant writers, without hesitation or shame, vividly bared their feelings about the American experience, using the artistic form with which they were most comfortable and familiar— the formulaic folk song. These compositions also reveal their authors to be from a region where, in comparison with China's northern urban centers, literary cultivation was not very sophisticated. For us today, it is exciting to learn that these folk rhymes express both the serious and the humorous side of the life of the early immigrants. Together with the Toisaan folk songs on America, these

Cantonese vernacular writings from Chinatown provide us with an authentic glimpse into the fascinating and diverse lives of the Chinese affected by the American experience at the turn of this century.

ONE

Immigration Blues

The Chinese Exclusion Act of 1882 opened an infamous
chapter in United States immigration history, one that
brought insurmountable hardship to the Chinese. The
moment that their ship docked at the San Francisco pier,
the Chinese immigrants were herded into the notorious
detention center known to all the Chinese as the "Muk
uk" (Mu wu), or "Wooden Barracks," to be processed
for immigration. Before 1910, detainees were sent to a
wooden building alongside the Pacific Mail Steamship
Company pier that was known as the "Tongsaan Matau"
(Tangshan Matou), the China Dock (now Pier 50 on the
San Francisco waterfront). Because of rampant corrup-
tion and the facility's poor physical condition, it ceased
to be used in 1910. Instead, the government put into
operation the newly built Angel Island Immigration
Station in San Francisco Bay to process immigrants and
returnees from Asia. This station was sometimes called
the Ellis Island of the West Coast.

At Angel Island, the Chinese had to submit to a battery of physical examinations and harsh interrogations. Those who passed were ferried to San Francisco to begin their new life; those who did not were deported back to China permanently. Detainees at the Wooden Barracks were not allowed to go beyond the compound or to meet any outside visitors. It was not uncommon to be detained in the Wooden Barracks for several weeks, even over a year, while awaiting processing. The facilities were minimal, without any consideration for privacy. Suicides were not unknown.

Many of the Chinese at the Angel Island Wooden Barracks wrote poems expressing their agony, frustration, anger, and despair. They would scribble the lines all over the walls of the barracks where they slept. In the 1930s, two detainees copied these scribbles and brought them to San Francisco. However, this genre of Chinese immigration poetry remained unknown to most people until recently.*

In 1940, a fire destroyed the administration building of the Angel Island Immigration Station, and the use of the facility was soon halted. Detainees were moved to another detention center in San Francisco. Barrack 37, the housing compound, survived the fire, but was forgotten for thirty years. Finally in the early 1970s, when the building was targeted for demolition, the Chinese scribbles on the walls caught the attention of the Chinese in San Francisco. Community efforts from Chinatown saved Barrack 37, and it has since become a historical site, augmented by an exhibit on the island's Chinese immigration history. Over 135 Wooden Barracks poems are extant today.

*See n. 73 of introduction for publication information.

The Cantonese folk rhymes on immigration in the 1911 anthology represent the earliest collection of published poems dealing with the Chinese immigration experience. They are different from the poems on the Wooden Barrack walls. Not only do these rhymes protest the harsh treatment at the Wooden Barracks; they also show that Angel Island with its Wooden Barracks was not a euphoric Ellis Island for the Chinese immigrants. Instead, it was a contradiction to the principles of liberty that testified to injustice. This criticism, so pronounced in these rhymes, reveals that the Chinese immigrants did have an appreciation of the American principles of justice and democracy. They expected to be treated on that level and they believed that they should be accorded such rights. This was, I believe, the first crude sign of their Americanization.

1   As soon as it is announced
          the ship has reached America:
     I burst out cheering,
          I have found precious pearls.
     How can I bear the detention upon arrival,
     Doctors and immigration officials refusing
          to let me go?
     All the abuse—
     I can't describe it with a pen.
     I'm held captive in a wooden barrack, like King Wen
          in Youli:*
     No end to the misery and sadness in my heart.

一話船到美。歡同得寶珠。
那堪抵埠受羈縻，醫生稅員未準紙
受太氣。筆尖難以紀。
板樓困入如羑里，無限凄涼心裡悲。

(一)一話：一說
(二)稅員：海關官員
(三)準：作「准」；未准紙：
    不發准許入境證件

JSGJ I.13b

*King Wen (ca. 1200 B.C.), the first ruler of the Zhou
dynasty, was detained in Youli for being an adversary
of the ruling Shang.

2   The moment I hear
          We've entered the port,
     I am all ready:
          my belongings wrapped in a bundle.
     Who would have expected joy to become sorrow:
     Detained in a dark, crude, filthy room?
     What can I do?
     Cruel treatment, not one restful breath of air,
     Scarcity of food, severe restrictions—all
          unbearable.
     Here even a proud man bows his head low.

一聞入港口。打起個伏包(一)。

誰知歡喜反爲愁。闇室受困更濁陋。

冇能較(二)。殘酷氣難哮。

缺食不堪嚴掣肘。英雄到此也垂頭。

(一) 伏：作「袱」

(二) 冇能較：沒法計較，無可奈何

JSGJ I.13b

3   In search of a pin–head gain,
    I was idle in an impoverished village.
    I've risked a perilous journey to come to the Flowery
        Flag Nation.
    Immigration officers interrogated me:
    And, just for a slight lapse of memory,
    I am deported, and imprisoned in this barren
        mountain.
    A brave man cannot use his might here,
    And he can't take one step beyond the confines.

欲菟蠅頭利。窮鄉沒作置。

乘危履險走花旗⁽一⁾。遇着稅員盤詰汝。

稍忘記。撥禁荒島裡。

好漢真無用武地。不能一步越雷池。

（一）花旗：美國

（二）稅員：參看歌#1

（三）撥：驅逐

JSGJ I.5a

4   At home I was in poverty,
        constantly worried about firewood and rice.
I borrowed money
        to come to Gold Mountain.
Immigration officers cross-examined me;
        no way could I get through.
Deported to this island,
        like a convicted criminal.
Here—
Mournful sighs fill the gloomy room.
A nation weak; her people often humiliated
Like animals, tortured and destroyed at others'
    whim.

家貧柴米患。貸本來金山(一)。
關員審問脫身難。撥往埃崙(二)如監犯(三)。
到此間。闇室長嗟嘆。
國弱被人多辱慢。儼然畜類任摧殘。

(一)金山：美國
(二)撥：參看歌#3
(三)埃崙：音譯「島」；
指天使島

JSGJ I.14a

5   Wooden barracks, all specially built;
It's clear they're detention cells.
We Chinese enter this country and suffer
All sorts of autocratic restrictions made at
   whim.
What a disappointment—
Cooped up inside an iron cage;
We have an impotent ambassador who cannot
   handle matters.
We knit our brows and cry for heaven gives no
   recourse for our suffering.

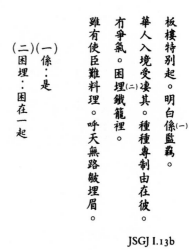

板樓特別起。明白係監羈。

華人入境受淒其。種種專制由在彼。

冇爭氣。困埋鐵籠裡。

雖有使臣難料理。呼天無路皺埋眉。

(一)
係：是

(二)
困埋：困在一起

JSGJ I.13b

6   The wooden cell is like a steel barrel.
    Firmly shut, not even a breeze can filter
        through.
    Over a hundred cruel laws, hard to list
        them all;
    Ten thousand grievances, all from the
        tortures day and night.
    Worry, and more worry—
    How can I sleep in peace or eat at ease?
    There isn't a cangue, but the hidden
        punishment is just as weighty.*
    Tears soak my clothes; frustration fills my
        bosom.

室板如鐵桶。嚴關不漏風。
百般苛例講唔窮(一)。朝夕被凌悲萬種。
憂忡忡。寢膳遑安用。
雖無枷鎖陰刑重。淚滿衣裳悶滿胸。

（一）唔窮：不盡

JSGJ I.14a

*A cangue consists of two locked wooden boards
with holes for the neck and hands. A convict wears it
around his neck, with his hands bound in front of him
and his feet in chains.

7   Dentention is called "awaiting review."
No letter or message can get through to me.
My mind's bogged down with a hundred frustrations
    and anxieties,
My mouth balks at meager meals of rice gruel.
O, what can I do?
Just when can I go ashore?
Imprisoned in a coop, unable to breathe,
My countrymen are made into a herd of cattle!

羈留名審候。信息不通透。

百般抑鬱在心頭。水飯一些難入口。

乜能較(一)。幾時得上埠(二)。

闇室監禁氣莫哮(三)。嗟我同胞作馬牛。

（一）乜能較：無奈何；參看歌 #2

（二）上埠：登岸進城

（三）氣莫哮：不能平靜休息

JSGJ I.14a

8   America, I have come and landed,
And am stranded here, for more than a year.
Suffering thousands upon thousands of
    mistreatments.
Is it in retribution for a past life that I
    deserve such defilement?
It is outrageous—
Being humiliated repeatedly by them.
I pray my country will become strong and
    even the score:
Send out troops, like Japan's war against
    Russia!*

JSGJ I.14a

*In the Russo-Japanese War of 1903, Japan defeated Russia in Manchuria, in northeastern China, and emerged from this war as a world power.

9　A weak nation can't speak up for herself.
　Chinese sojourners have come to a foreign
　　country.
　Detained, put on trial, imprisoned in a hillside
　　building;
　If deposition doesn't exactly match: the case is dead
　　and in a bind.
　No chance for release.
　My fellow countrymen cry out injustice:
　The sole purpose is strict exclusion, to deport
　　us all back to Hong Kong.
　Pity my fellow villagers and their flood of tears.

國弱真難講。華僑到異邦。
阻留候審困山房。(一)供一不符案死綁。(二)
總唔放。同胞呼寬枉。
志在嚴禁撥返港。(三)可憐梓里淚汪汪。

（一）山房：天使島移民拘留所背山面海，
　　　　故曰「山房」
（二）供：口供
（三）撥：參看歌#3

JSGJ I.14a

10 The mighty power rescinds her treaty;
The weak race suffers oppression from the mighty.
I am jailed unjustly across the bay,
Enduring the unendurable tyranny of immigration
   officials.
Doors: firmly shut.
Guards and officers: watching me closely, like wolves.
News and letters: not permitted.
O, it's hard to bear the hundred cruel regulations
   they devise at will.

JSGJ I.13b

11   American laws, more ferocious than tigers:
Many are the people jailed inside wooden walls,
Detained, interrogated, tortured,
Like birds plunged into an open trap—
    What suffering!
To whom can I complain of the tragedy?
I shout to Heaven, but there is no way out!
Had I only known such difficulty in passing
    the Golden Gate . . .
Fed up with this treatment, I regret my journey here.

美例奇於虎。人困板壁多。

所留候審受擊磨。鳥入樊籠折太陸(一)。

慘莫訴。呼天嘆無路。

關過金門難若此。飽嘗況味悔奔波。

（一）折陸：參看歌#8

JSGJ I.13b

12   So, liberty is your national principle;
     Why do you practice autocracy?
     You don't uphold justice, you Americans,
     You detain me in prison, guard me closely.
     Your officials are wolves and tigers,
     All ruthless, all wanting to bite me.
     An innocent man implicated, such an injustice!
     When can I get out of this prison and free
        my mind?

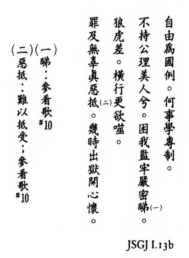

JSGJ I.13b

13 Fellow countrymen, four hundred million
    strong;
Many are great, with exceptional talents.
We want to come to the Flowery Flag Nation
    but are barred;
The Golden Gate firmly locked, without even
    a crack to crawl through.
This moment—
Truly deplorable is the imprisonment.
Our hearts ache in pain and shame;
Though talented, how can we put on wings and
    fly past the barbarians?

同胞四萬萬。豪傑在其間。
花旗(一)欲入被他攔。緊鎖金門無路趨。
這一番。拘囚眞可恨。
縱有奇才心痛根。怎能插翼越夷蠻。

（一）
花旗：參看歌#3

JSGJ I.5b

14   I roam America undocumented.
     White men blackmail me with many demands.
     I say one thing, and they, another;
     I want to complain of injustice, but my tongue
         stutters.
     At a loss for words—
     I wrack my brain for a solution, to no avail.
     Thrown into a prison cage, I cannot fly away.
     Don't you think this is cruel? Don't you think
         this is cruel?

遊美因冇册⁽一⁾。洋人多索勒。

我講南時佢講北⁽二⁾。欲訴寃情又語塞。

口嘿嘿。思量無計策。

被困牢籠飛不得。汝話奇刻唔奇刻⁽三⁾。

（一）册：指「册紙」：身份證明文件；

冇册：冇證件

（二）佢：他

（三）話：説，認爲，覺得

JSGJ I.13b

15 I am a man of heroic deeds;
I am a man with pride and dignity.
My bosom encompasses the height of Heaven
and the brilliance of Earth;
Everywhere they know me as a truly noble
man.
In search of wealth—
Greed led me on the road to Gold Mountain.
Denied landing upon reaching the shore, I am
filled with rage.
With no means to pass the border, what can a
person do?

處世豪傑士。堂堂大丈夫。

高明天地胸全羅。四處傳名眞君子。

欲愛富。貪走金山路。

抵岸難登氣滿肚。越界無策奈誰何。

JSGJ I.5b

16　Stay at home and lose opportunities;
　　A hundred considerations lead me to sojourn
　　　　in Mexico.
　　Political parties are like wolves and tigers eliminating
　　　　each other;
　　Hatred and prejudice against foreigners take away our
　　　　property and many lives.
　　Unable to stay on—
　　I sneak across the border to the American side,
　　But bump into an immigration officer who sternly
　　　　throws the book at me
　　And orders my expulsion back to China.

守家多失策。百謀方旅墨。
政黨相持狼虎革。仇視外人財命索。
唔棲得(一)。偷關過美域。
撞着稅員嚴拉冊(二)。令我回華申逐客。

（一）
稅員：參看歌#1

（二）
拉冊：審查「冊紙」及拘捕無
冊紙者；參看歌#14

JSGJ II.11a

17 A transient living beneath a stranger's
   fence.
   Cruelties increase day by day.
   Though innocent, I am arrested and thrown
      in jail;
   Pathetic the lonely bachelors stranded in a
      foreign land.
   O, let's all go home.
   Spare ourselves of this mighty tyrant.
   The outside world may be entertaining at times;
   But life at home is just as bustling.

寄居人籬下。苛刻日日加。
無辜被拘禁監衙。羈留異地憐孤寡。
歸去罷。免受他強霸。
外國世界雖樂也。故園風景却繁華。

JSGJ II.40b

TWO

Lamentations of Stranded Sojourners

Economic hardship is the theme of the rhymes contained in this section. In recruiting Cantonese to work as laborers in America's West, Western capitalists preached the promise and glory of economic advancement. The possibility of attaining a better life was an irresistible temptation in southeastern China during the mid-nineteenth century, as many of the inhabitants of the region had been reduced to a marginal existence by natural and human disasters. Therefore, the news of economic opportunity was a welcome relief, and the discovery of gold in California only further encouraged the desperate Cantonese natives to rush to the United States. The promise of a steady income by working on the construction of the transcontinental railroads was also readily accepted by these impoverished men. Thus, they made the journey, thousands of miles across the perilous Pacific Ocean, pursuing their Gold Mountain Dream of success, a dream not too different from that of their European immigrant counterparts.

The Chinese immigrants worked hard at their jobs. They reclaimed California land and laid the foundation for the state to become the salad bowl of America. They mined claims that had been abandoned by white miners, paying a hefty foreign miners' tax. They worked on railroad construction, handling the most dangerous assignments, at a cost of thousands of lives. The wages they were paid, however, were lower than those of white workers. When they struck to demand better pay, their employer cut off their food supplies and the white workers did not support them. In the winter season, they lived and worked literally in the snow while laying track through the Sierra mountains. An avalanche could claim many lives without warning. When spring finally arrived, the bodies would emerge from the melting snow, intact, still holding picks and shovels, as a frozen testimony to their hardships.

Hardship and labor in the United States were an accepted reality for these Cantonese men, but the rampant racial prejudice of American society only made their lives more miserable. Even in urban San Francisco, their economic opportunities were limited. Many became disillusioned upon realizing that, after years of toiling in pain, there was not one sign of relief. Increasing their plight was the agony and frustration that they felt when they recognized the fact that their journey to America was not made just for themselves. Their sense of duty to their families back in China, who depended on them for survival, became an ever-present reminder, pushing them to the edge of desperation. A man's ability to achieve economic success and to provide for his family was the ultimate judgment of his success in the American sojourn. Anything less than that would be considered a failure. Thus, the most poignant reference in these rhymes about hardship is not to the actual hardship or physical labor, but to the lack of economic reward. When their labor went unrewarded, many of these men became resigned to fate and disillusioned; others still desperately continued trying. Regardless of their differing responses to this harsh reality, all were haunted by the Gold Mountain Dream.

18   Dispirited by life in my village home,
      I make a journey specially to the United States
          of America.
      Separated by mountains and passes, I feel an
          extreme anxiety and grief;
      Rushing about east and west does me no good.
      Turning in all directions—
      An ideal opportunity has yet to come.
      If fate is indeed Heaven's will, what more can
          I say?
      'Tis a disgrace to a man's pride and dignity.

失志居鄉黨。特來遊美邦。
關山阻隔極悽惶。東走西奔無善狀。
遍四方。未逢佳景況。
命實由天真譽講(一)。男兒應愧貌堂堂。

（一）
譽講：難說

JSGJ II.12a

19   Born into a rotten life,
Coming or going, all without leaving my mark.
Even after leaving the village for a foreign
    country,
Running about east and west, I've gained nothing.
Everything's turned upside down;
It's more disconcerting being away from home.
I have gone to the four corners of the world;
Alas, I am neither at ease while resting nor
    happy while moving.

一生條命薄。來去都冇作(一)。
縱使離鄉往外國。東走西奔無所獲。
陰陽錯。出門更落索(二)。
轉過天涯四個角。居弗安兮行弗樂。

(一) 冇作：沒有成就
(二) 落索：孤伶失意

JSGJ II.12b

20   Pitiful is the twenty-year sojourner,
     Unable to make it home.
     Having been everywhere—north, south, east,
        west—
     Always obstacles along the way, pain knitting
        my brows.
     Worried, in silence.
     Ashamed, wishes unfulfilled.
     A reflection on the mirror, a sudden fright:
        hair, half frost-white.
     Frequent letters from home, all filled with much
        complaint.

對鏡乍驚頭半白。家書屢接頻交謫。

遍歷東南又西北。所爲輒阻常蹙額。

愁默默。自慙志不得。

廿年悲作客。猶未返故宅。

JSGJ II.11b

21 Come to think of it, what can I really say?
    Thirty years living in the United States—
    Why has life been so miserable and I, so frail?
    I suppose it's useless to expect to go home.
    My heart aches with grief;
    My soul wanders around aimlessly.
    Unable to make a living here, I'll try it in the East,
    With a sudden change of luck, I may make it back to
        China.

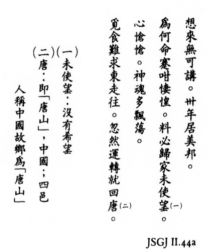

JSGJ II.44a

22   Stranded in a lodge: a delay;
Old debts up to my ears: here to stay.
No sign of relief, only a pain stealing through
    my heart,
And nagged by worry for my aged parents.
I want to go home;
But what can I do without money in my purse?
Determined to shape up and shake loose, I move
    elsewhere;
But I am still stuck with rotten luck, as life only
    gets worse.

逗遛羇旅郎。依舊滿身債。
毫無振作暗傷懷。每念高堂年紀邁。
欲歸計。囊中有文解。(一)
發奮圖強來他徙。仍然屯塞事無諧。

(一)有文：沒有一分錢

JSGJ II.11b

23   I have walked to the very ends of the earth,
A dusty, windy journey.
I've toiled and I'm worn out, all for a miserable lot.
Nothing is ideal when I am down and out.
I think about it day and night—
Who can save a fish out of water?
From far away, I worry for my parents, my wife,
    my boy:
Do they still have enough firewood, rice, salt, and
    cooking oil?

走盡天涯路。風塵跋涉多。
勞勞碌碌為窮途。景遇未逢真不妥。
朝夕思。憑誰救涸鮒。
遠念高堂妻共子。柴米油鹽尚有無。

JSGJ II.12a

24 Toiling in pain, east and west, all in vain;
Hurrying about, north and south, still more
rushing.
What can a person do with a life full of mishap?
Searching, scheming, on all four sides, not
one good lead in sight.
Eyes brimming with tears:
O, I just can't get rid of the misery.
My belly is full of frustration and grievance;
When life is at low ebb, I suffer dearly.

東西徒勤苦。南北更奔波。
命途多舛奈誰何。四邊求謀無好路。
眼悚悚。淒涼有計度。(一)
抑鬱牢騷堆滿肚。人生當晦受磋磨。

（一）有計：沒有辦法

JSGJ II.11a

25 Drifting around, all over the place,
Seeking food everywhere, in all four directions.
Turning east, going west, always on an
    uncertain road;
Toiling, rushing about, much ado for nothing.
Fed by wind and frost,
I search for wealth, but all in vain.
If fate indeed has excluded me so, what more can
    I say?
After years of sojourn, I sigh in fear.

遍地飄流蕩。覓食走四方。

東轉西至路渺茫。勞碌奔馳寬太柱。

飽風霜。求財空虛望。

命裡唔湊真謷講(二)。客途歲月嗟悽惶。

（一）
唔湊：不吻合

（二）
謷講：參看歌 #18

26　Look at that face in the mirror:
　　My appearance so completely changed.
　　Hair white as frost, long beard hanging;
　　Disheartening are the bald spots sparkling
　　　　like stars.
　　Old age has arrived.
　　No longer is my face young and handsome.
　　Without my noticing, I am already over forty.
　　Shame is toiling in hardship, across the vast
　　　　and distant oceans.

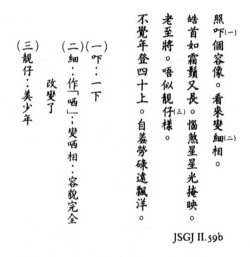

照吓(一)個容像。看來變細(二)相。
皓首如霜鬚又長。惱煞星星光掩映。
老至將。唔似靓仔(三)樣。
不覺年登四十上。自羞勞碌遠飄洋。

（一）吓：一下
（二）細：作「哂」；變哂相：容貌完全
　　　改變了
（三）靓仔：美少年

27 My ambition wouldn't allow me to stay cooped up
in humility.
I took a raft and sailed the seas.
Rising early at dawn, with the stars above me,
I traveled deep into the night, the moon my
companion.
Who could have known it would be a journey full of
rain and snow?
Winds pierced through my bones.
Hugging a blanket, my thighs trembling.
I wish to buy a fox-fur coat, but lack the
money—
Right now I don't have the means even to fight
the cold!

志不甘蟄屈。乘桴浮海出。
早起披星夜戴月。誰識客途多雨雪。
風刺骨。擁衾雙股慄。
欲購狐裘銀又缺。此際禦冬真無術。

JSGJ II.14b

28   The Flowery Flag Nation is deep in frost and heavy
       with snow.
   No one can withstand its winter without a fur
       coat.
   Traveling is not at all like staying at home:
   In thin clothing on wintry days, my shoulders and
       arms shrug and shiver in the cold.
   Even if you are brave and strong,
   The fierce wind will bend your back into a bow.
   Prepare a cotton-padded gown and rush it to me!
   Don't make this distant traveler wait anxiously
       for the journeying geese!*

花旗霜雪重。非裘莫禦冬。

出外居家總不同。衫少歲寒肩膊聳。

雖壯勇。風猛腰亦拱。

整備綿袍早遞送。免教遠客盼征鴻。

JSGJ II.14a

*Migratory geese—a metaphor for news messengers.

29 Men on the remote frontier, all terrified:
In autumn, north winds begin to blow.
Sojourners from faraway places share the same
thought:
O, how can this little bit of clothing be enough
in deep frost and heavy snow?
Once winter comes—
A fur coat is needed all the more in the
freezing cold.
I can buy one at a clothing store,
But it's not the same as the one sewn by my dear wife
or my mother.

（一）當：作「擋」

遠塞人心悚。因秋起朔風。
退方旅客念相同。衫少怎當(一)霜雪重。
一交冬。更需裘禦凍。
服店雖能加購用。奚如慈母與妻縫。

JSGJ II.15a

30 Life is like a vast, long dream.
    Why grieve over poverty?
    A contented life soothes ten thousand matters.
    Value the help from other people.
    In all earnest, just endure:
    You can forget about cold and hunger, as you
      see them often.
    After lasting through winter's chill and snow's
      embrace,
    You will find joy in life when happiness comes
      and sorrow fades.

處世若大夢。胡爲怨恨窮。

人生安份萬事通。玉汝於成雖珍重。

耐忍衷。見慣忘飢凍。

捱過歲寒和雪擁。苦盡甜來樂在中。

JSGJ I.20b

31 A brave man meeting an untimely adversity,
All day long, unable to eat or sleep.
Rushing about over ten thousand miles,
deep in sorrow,
Every hour, every minute, mind and body
toil in pain.
Heaven's will is extreme!
This big roc wants to spread its wings.*
Yet scores are not evened up; the mind is not
at ease.
Alas, I can't rest in peace, I just can't rest
in peace.

烈士運逢逆。終朝忘寢食。

萬里奔馳愁戚戚。時刻勞心兼勞力。

天意極。大鵬就振翼。

前仇未報眞唔値。難安息兮難安息。

JSGJ I.20a

* "Big roc," an allusion from *Zhuang zi*, commonly refers to a person who is about to seek out a great future.

32   To be hard pressed by poverty is truly disgusting.
     Yet it's all due to fate.
     Since antiquity, great men have often had to contend
          with adversity;
     Remember, the cycle of life is Heaven's way.
     So there's no need to complain.
     All matters will turn around in the end, they
          always do;
     One day, Heaven's eyes will no longer wink at me,*
     And we'll go back to South China with enough
          money.

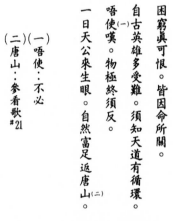

JSGJ I.20a

   *A Cantonese expression meaning positive retribu-
tion for a good deed.

33 In dire need of food and clothing,
    I took my chances and came to Mexico alone.*
    Savages rob and loot with frequent violence.
    I ask Heaven: Why is there hatred against the
        yellow race?
    On a journey,
    It's hard to go anywhere without money.
    With deep sorrow we Chinese sojourners must
        face many calamities,
    Wondering when we can expect to go home in
        triumph and in grace.

只爲衣食窮。挺身來呂宋。

番奴掠劫屢行兇。問天何事厭黃種。

旅途中。無錢身難動。

深惜華僑遭劫重。那知方許望旋東。

（一）呂宋：照歌中内容，不應指

菲律賓，該爲墨西哥

JSGJ II.41a

*For the Chinese in America, *Leuisung* refers to the
Philippines or Mexico, or sometimes Cuba, probably
because Spanish is spoken in these places. Here, the
term refers to Mexico, as the poem depicts the turmoil
of the Mexican Revolution of 1910, as also seen in
song 16.

34 Since coming to the frontier land,
    I have taken all kinds of abuse from the
        barbarians.
    I have come across the horizon to the Flowery
        Flag Nation;
    The surroundings still fill me with thoughts
        of home.
    Don't despair:
    All we need is profit and money.
    Should our purses be stuffed with gold,
    We'll pick out a date and have our homebound
        whip ready.

自到邊疆地。受盡番奴欺。

天涯走過至花旗(一)。觸景依然懷故里。

莫傷氣。祇爭財與利。

黃金揶入荷包裡。整定歸鞭有日期。

(一) 花旗：參看歌 #3

JSGJ I.12a

THREE

Lamentations of Estranged Wives

The separation of husband and wife was the most difficult emotional issue for the Chinese immigrants in the United States. Traditional Cantonese practices and unjust American immigration practices made it impossible for wives to come to the United States with their husbands unless the latter were of the merchant class. Hence, Chinatown became a "bachelor society"—a community of married men who lived without their wives—and their home villages turned into a land of widows, as married women had to live without the companionship of their spouses. Since the Cantonese practice was to make sure that a man was married before he left home to earn a living, many of these women were newlyweds when their husbands left home. These women knew little about America, known to them as Gold Mountain or Flowery Flag, where their spouses had gone to spend years of their life in toil and hardship. They knew it only as a faraway place that took away their husbands, in exchange for a seasonal remittance.

Patiently they waited for the husbands to return; many waited in vain, as their dear ones vanished in that foreign land without a trace. For some of the men, the return home was in a box that contained only their bones, shipped back home by the charity arm of their district association in the United States for a proper and final burial.

The rhymes in this section that are written in the wife's persona are laden with immense emotion. I have divided them into two groups. The rhymes in the larger group focus on the woman's feelings about separation. Her need for companionship and the lack of it led to great agony, frustration, and pain. Her world is seen as a domestic one, in which she lives for her husband's presence. In his absence, her life is miserable, unfulfilled, and meaningless, as she lacks an independent life of her own. The return of her husband from Gold Mountain rejuvenates her; his prolonged absence only withers her prematurely.

The other rhymes comprise only a minority. In them, the marriage of an intelligent woman to an inept man is looked at from the wife's point of view. In traditional China, the bride was not allowed a voice in her marriage. The matchmaker proposed and arranged the marriage, which was actually between two families; the parents of the bride and groom made the decisions. The two families' social and economic status, not the individual persons involved, had to be compatible. If a couple was poorly matched, it would lead to much grief and sorrow for both husband and wife, but more so for the woman, since the man was allowed to take another wife, whereas society scorned the woman who divorced and remarried. Interestingly enough, in these rhymes the protest against arranged marriage is not based on the traditional standard of class compatibility, but on individuality. Probably influenced by the modern Western concept of individual compatibility, this rebellious notion is at odds with the traditional Chinese notion that the woman should never stress her own intelligence over a man's. She might resent being married to an inferior man, but her duty was to make the situation more tolerable for herself by practicing the traditional feminine virtues, or else die with that unresolved resentment. In these rhymes, however, the woman's voice emphasizes individual liberty, as she seeks conjugal compatibility by divorcing her inferior husband and marrying someone else—something unheard of in early twentieth-century China.

35 Husband: his foolishness is second to none.
Life indeed is tragic for the woman.
Seek a divorce, like an American?
But the Chinese do not work things out
   in that way!
A belly full of resentment,
At the sight of him, eyes burst out in flames.
What evil deed in my previous life made me
   married to you?
Why me? Why did I end up with such a fool?

婿蠢真無比。婦也實傷悲。

欲將離異學花旗。可恨華人無此理。

一肚氣。眼見火就起。(一)

幾世修行嫁着爾。何故遇此混屯兒。

（一）眼火起：眼睛冒火

JSGJ I.40a

36 Husband: so dumb, second to none;
Wife: wounded with deep resentment.
Foolish and naive, he doesn't know when
    to have fun;
It's a real bore to be with him at any moment.
Alas! is this called fate?
I am disgusted with the family, everyone.
Had I followed the Western practice and
    made my own choice,
Never, never would I have agreed to wed a moron.

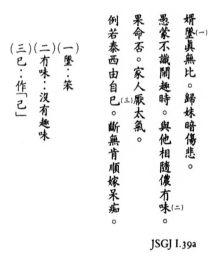

婿墜真無比。歸妹暗傷悲。

愚蒙不識鬧趣時。與他相隨儂冇味(二)。

果命否。家人厭太氣。

例若泰西由自巳(三)。斷無肯順嫁呆痴。

（一）墜：：笨

（二）冇味：：沒有趣味

（三）巳：：作「己」

JSGJ I.39a

37 I ended up with a simpleton husband;
The fun and games in life, all betrayed.
Just look at him: stupid, clumsy, like a lump
of clay,
A good-for-nothing, skilled in neither craft
nor trade.
O, my whole life is wronged—
I resent the red string binding us together by
mistake.*
If, by chance, this marriage can be dissolved,
I would be most happy to throw out another bouquet.†

湊着庸愚婿。風流負却細(一)。
見佢呆蠢似圍坭。工商唔曾熟一藝。
屈該世。赤繩怨錯繫。
設若婚姻能拆解。花毬再拋也開懷。

（一）細：：作「哂」；負哂：：完全辜負了

JSGJ I.40b

*"Red string" is a metaphor for a nuptial relation-
ship.
†"To throw out a bouquet" is a reference to the
popular legend of Wang Baochuan (translated as *Lady
Precious Stream* by S. I. Hsiung), who threw out an em-
broidery bouquet to the public to select her marital
mate. Xue Rengui, a poor soul, caught her bouquet,
and she married him despite his poverty.

38 Unexpectedly I heard Husband say that
    He's about to study abroad.
    My mind is confused, as tangled up as hemp
        fibers.
    So we have money, but what do I care!
    Who wouldn't be afraid—
    To live like a widow in my young age?
    If it's not proper for me to tag along,
    What ingenious scheme can I dream up to keep
        him to me, close and dear?

乍聞夫婿話。遊學去歐亞。

令奴心事亂如麻。即使有錢都係假。

誰唔怕。青春生守寡。

倘若隨行失大雅。憑何妙計挽留他。

JSGJ I.23a

39 Husband says he's going to Gold Mountain
And doesn't listen to my pleas.
In the still of night, full of thoughts, I cannot
rest my eyes.
Standing before the dresser alone, I face a
grieving reflection.
I wonder
What man doesn't treasure a lover's bond?
Youth, once gone, will never return;
We may become rich, but wealth is really
nothing!

郎話去金山。總唔聽奴諫。

靜夕思量難閉眼。粧台獨立對愁顏。

想一番。情義誰不恨(一)。

青春過了唔再返。縱然富貴也當閒。

（一）不恨：不愛惜

JSGJ I.51b

40   The sailing date approaches in quick pace.
Husband will be off to Gold Mountain.
At first I thought it was all fun and excitement;
Who would see it, in our youthful years, as a
    cruel separation?
But suddenly—
An endless remorse, aroused by his parting.
Husband says he must go; I plead: don't go so soon;
Don't leave this young woman all by her lonesome
    self, grief-stricken.

君話出門去且慢。免教寂寞怨紅顏。

怎陣間。離情無限恨。

當初只話鬧風繁。誰料青春生拆散。

船期催緊板。夫婿往金山。

JSGJ I.23a

41 Dear Husband, you mention a journey to Europe
and America;
Side by side in bed, softly I speak words of
advice:
Once you have made some small gain, hurry home;
Be on guard, there are vices of which you may not
even be aware.
By all means, remember:
Years go by in the twinkling of an eye.
Work hard, earn gold and silver, prepare for our
later years;
And, at this moment, we still don't have an heir.

君話遊歐美。枕畔細喁噯。

蠅頭覓利早歸期。切勿邪行唔覺起。

須緊記。轉瞬多歲紀。

勤取金銀妨晚裡。眼前還未有孩兒。

（一）
妨：作「防」

JSGJ II.10a

42 Exuberant willows, playful along the riverside;
A distant journey, revealed in the young woman's
   eyes.
Her mothlike brows are locked in sorrow; trees
   become a blur.
With no sight of her husband, sorrow besieges her.
Remembering the peak of Wu Mountain,*
No longer possible, the dreams of clouds and rain.†
Great grief and resentment are sown by separation.
All in the cries of orioles, the calls of swallows.

幾多幽恨離情種。都在鶯啼燕語中。

娥眉愁鎖樹朦朧。未見君子憂忡忡。

憶巫峰。難成雲雨夢。

柳色堤邊弄。佳人遠目送。

JSGJ 1.27a

*"Wu Mountain" is a metaphor for a lovers' ren-
dezvous or the act of sexual intimacy. It originated
from a Han dynasty myth about Emperor Wu (reigned
140–86 B.C.).
†"Clouds and rain" alludes to the act of sexual
intimacy.

43   Once you sing the parting song,
I'll end up living in loneliness and pain.
Ten thousand miles of clouds and mountains
    tear apart the bliss of our love,
While my life is young and vital and in full
    spring.
Husband is on a distant journey—
Who wouldn't be worried?
Even if he should come back in triumph and
    grace,
The tender years of my life will have all but gone
    to waste.

縱然衣錦回鄉井。畢竟拋荒妾妙齡。

壻長征。問誰唔著緊(一)。

雲山萬里隔恩情。奴況青春纔值令。

驪歌君一詠。儂就苦零丁。

（一）著緊：著急

JSGJ I.22b

44　After we wed,
　　I am lacquer and husband, glue.*
　　At sixteen my life is in full blossom;
　　A hundred delights fill us to our hearts' content.
　　Sadly I am forsaken,
　　Living for a long time in solitude.
　　The way parents-in-law behave is hard to explain.
　　O, what can I do but live through these days of
　　　　prolonged delay?

JSGJ I.42b

*"Glue and lacquer" is a conventional metaphor
used for an ideal marital relationship.

45   Enjoining the words thousands of times:
     Deep is our love as we share the pillow.
     I ask Husband: you're leaving now, but when
       will you return?
     Take pity on your wife living like a swan, all
       alone.
     Quietly I sigh.
     Alone in bed I cannot close my eyes.
     I can't stop the fleeting years;
     Letters of love, soaked with tears, all sent to you,
       my dear.

致囑言千萬。情濃在枕間。

問郎今別幾時還。憐奴獨處如孤雁。

暗自嘆。孤眠難入眼。

歲月催人無計挽。淚灑情書達君顏。

JSGJ I.28b

46　Since you've sojourned to America, Husband,
My heart aches for you all the time.
Unable to share my feelings, my brows are
　　besieged with sorrow;
I grieve that we're at opposite ends of the
　　earth.
Mourning at midnight,
I cannot fall asleep in the gauze-tented bed.
Thinking, wondering, O, who is the trusted
　　friend?
Who will deliver my message to the Flowery Flag
　　Nation?

籌度孰爲賢知己。代奴傳語到花旗。

幽懷難遮鎖愁眉。惱恨天涯隔兩地。

午夜悲。羅幃難入寐。

自君遊歐美。妾每心記記。

JSGJ I.50a

47   We had been wed for only a few nights;
Then you left me for Gold Mountain.
For twenty long years you haven't returned.
For this, I embrace only resentment in my bedroom;
Heaving a sigh
For the faraway sojourner who hasn't come home.
Everything brings me sorrow; I no longer care about
    my appearance,
Endless longing for you leads only to streams of
    falling tears.

洞房方幾晚。離別去金山。
廿年咁久未見還。令我閨幃空抱恨。
一聲嘆。遠遊駕莫返。
覩物生愁容懶扮。相思無限淚潸潸⁽²⁾。

（二）（一）
潸潸⁝咁⁝
⁝作這塵
「漕漕」

JSGJ I.51a

48　I count on my fingers: a year is about to end.
In the embroidery room, a young woman laments:
I am still somewhat young—
Yet time passes ever so quickly, in the blink
　　of an eye,
Gone and never to return;
No one can detain it.
Enjoy life when the time is right, don't ever delay.
Alas, no thanks to Husband, who has yet to come
　　home.

屈指年將晚。繡閣佳人嘆。

算來還有幾朱顏。光陰易過如斬眼(一)。

去唔返。幾多人難挽。

行樂及時唔好慢。虧奴夫婿未曾還。

（一）
斬眼：眨眼

JSGJ I.34b

49   The pair of mandarin ducks has been split apart;*
      The rouge-faced woman is left with a broken heart.
      How she regrets urging Husband to go to the
          Golden Gate.
      So many oceans, so many mountains—her spirit
          dies while she waits.
      Without a moment of peace—
      Youth goes away swiftly.
      Disheartening surroundings, a chaotic mind,
      How can she bear the full moon in the still of the
          night!†

觀物傷情心緒亂。何堪宵靜月圓圓。

刻難安。青春容易轉。

悔教夫婿往金門。重水重山魂望斷。

拆散鴛鴦伴。紅顏切胆肝。

JSGJ II.53b

    *A pair of either mandarin ducks or lovebirds is a
metaphor for a man and woman deeply in love.
    †"Full moon" is a literary allusion for the reunion of
lovers, family members, or friends.

50   Husband is in North America.
He leaves me so easily for some gain!
This makes me lonely, as I guard the scented
    bedroom by my lonesome self,
Giving up the gaiety of life at the age of
    twenty-two!
It's so frustrating.
This cold bedding keeps me from sleep.
I light the lamp, and again write him a letter
    from home,
Dear love, I ask, have you decided when to
    return?

良人在北美。重利輕別離。
令奴寂寞守香閨。屈了風流年廿二。
真激氣。衾寒難入寐。
桃燈又寫家書寄。問郎曾否定歸期。

（二）（一）
　　屈：辜負
（二）激氣：令人惱怒

JSGJ II.52b

51 Husband is stranded in a travelers' inn;
The rouge-faced woman, restless in her sleep,
Drafts a letter and asks the geese to take it to
   the Golden Gate;*
In it she pours out her deep feelings:
Dear love, please read on,
Our happy days are few.
Hurry, hurry home to share my pillow.
Spare me from growing cold and lonely under
   our jade-green quilt.

良人羈旅館。紅顏寢不安。

修書勞雁往金門。內寫衷情恁一欵。

請郎看。風流日子短。

快快來歸同枕伴。免奴翠被獨生寒。

JSGJ II.36a

* "Geese," see song 28.

52   Pressing poverty led to desperation;
      And Husband took off to Gold Mountain.
      It's been three years, or is it five, and I haven't
         seen him come home.
      Many times I write and ask the geese to deliver
         my letters to him:*
      O, far away from home,
      Pity the mandarin ducks torn apart by separation.†
      How can I get you back to cheer me up?
      Just come home, rich or poor, I simply don't care
         anymore!

怎　隔　三　因
得　鄉　年　窮
回　關　五　催
家　○　載　緊
慰　鴛　未　板
妾　鴦　見　○
恨　憐　還　良
○　拆　○　人
有　散　每　往
無　○　作　金
銀　　　迴　山
兩　　　文　○
亦　　　書
當　　　寄
閒　　　雁
○　　　○

JSGJ 1.23b

*"Geese," see song 28.
†"Mandarin ducks," see song 49.

53 Husband stays in a foreign land;
His suffering there leaves me grief-stricken.
Idle, sitting alone with knitted brows, I count:
Alas, over twenty years of my precious youth
have gone to waste.
Long sighs and long resignation—
Unable to sleep, I toss and turn.
Distant cries of geese arouse my melancholic
solitude;*
Many times, I dream of flying to the Flowery
Flag Nation.

郎君居異地。難情動妾悲。

無聊獨坐鎖雙眉。屈指韶光虛廿幾。

長歔欷。展轉難成寐。

恍惚雁聲愁觸起。幾回飛夢到花旗。

JSGJ I.51a

* "Geese," see song 28. Here they also symbolize the
migratory return of a sojourner.

54 A mere mention of Husband's journey—
A journey one thousand miles away from our
    bedroom—
And my heart is shattered into bits and pieces.
What young woman indeed is willing to sleep alone?
Grief and resentment, all piled up.
A pair of mandarin ducks, separated in two places.*
Let me ask you, my young peers in rouge:
How would you feel if you were severed from
    your husband?

JSGJ I.23a

*"Mandarin ducks," see song 49.

55 Dear husband, ever since you sojourned in a
    foreign land,
I've lost interest in all matters.
All day long, I stay inside the bedroom, my
    brows knitted;
Ten thousand thoughts bring me endless remorse.
In grief, in silence.
I cannot fall asleep on my lonely pillow.
Over the walls comes neighbors' laughter,
    piercing through my ears, vexing me with envy.
No thanks to you I alone must endure this misery.

自君遊異地。百事冇心機(一)。
蘭房終日鎖雙眉。萬種尋思愁莫已。
暗傷悲。孤枕難成寐。
惱煞隔墻笑徹耳。虧奴獨自嘆凄其。

（一）冇心機：沒有興趣

JSGJ I.23a

56   Fond thoughts of my man: a million emotions.
     My husband, a sojourner in Gold Mountain.
     Pity this lonesome rouge-faced young woman:
     I can live through the day, but not the night.
     In my embroidery room,
     Misery, with no end in sight.
     The sixteen-year-old Seung Ngo is made into a lonely
        swan.*
     Disheartened by a parting song, my tears quietly flow.

二八嫦娥如孤雁。忍聽驪歌淚暗彈。

綉房間。淒涼無可恨(一)。

可憐寂寞咁紅顏。得過日時難過晚。

懷人情千萬。夫壻客金山。

（一）
恨：作「限」

JSGJ I.24b

*In early Chinese mythology, Seung Ngo (Chang E
or Heng E), wife of Hau Yu (Hou Yi) who shot down
nine suns, stole the elixir of life and fled to the moon. In
popular literature, Chang E symbolizes a woman with
goddess-like beauty.

57 Husband has gone to a country far away.
The sorrows of separation are manifold in kind.
The bedroom is desolate; the quilt, chilly.
How can a single pillow be my mate in my lonely
    sleep?
My restless sleep?
With emotions suspended, depression lingers on.
I am thinking of my man, who hasn't yet returned
    from the ends of the earth;
I look up, and the moon, so round and full, brings
    me insurmountable frustration.*

懷念天涯人未轉。舉頭惱煞月團圓。

睡不安。情牽難解悶。

羅幃寂靜嘆襟寒。孤枕獨眠誰作伴。

君適他邦遠。離愁幾百般。

JSGJ I.28a

* "Full moon," see song 49.

58   Where is my husband now?
Before the vanity, I no longer care to paint my
   brows.
Spring catkins from the fields fly in through the
   curtains;
Orioles' cries startle and frustrate me.
O, silly me—
I cannot sleep with only a pillow.
Aroused by the sorrow of parting, a sorrow without
   an end,
I longingly recall plucking willow branches at the
   Farewell Pavilion.*

離愁觸起情何已。回憶長亭折柳枝。

陌頭飛絮入羅幃。惱煞鶯啼驚妾耳。

心癡癡。孤枕難成寐。

夫婿棲何地。臨粧懶畫眉。

JSGJ I.27a

   *"Plucking willow branches at the Farewell Pavi-
lion" is a literary allusion to a woman bidding fare-
well to her journeying lover/husband. The refer-
ence was popularized in the *West Chamber Romance*
(*Xixiang ji*), a Yuan dynasty drama based on a Tang
dynasty tale of premarital love.

59   I have finished my needlework for the night.
My mood is as chaotic as hemp fibers.
My blossoming years have been wrongly wasted
And I cannot even share with you the parting
     sorrow, a sorrow so immense in my mind.
A heart left dangling.
One day is three autumns.
Privately I pray Heaven to grant me this wish:
Let my husband come home early and in triumph.

今宵刀剪罷。情緒亂如麻。
却因喜負妾年華。滿腹離愁難共話。
心掛掛。一日三秋也。
竊願天緣能可假。等君衣錦早還家。

JSGJ I.28b

60   Youth is a blossom, a fleeting span.
How can you take leave for a distant place?
I grieve that I have no wings to fly by your
    side.*
Alone, hugging the scented quilt, I endure the
    sleepless nights.
I mourn, in silence.
A cold breeze comes through the curtains.
In melancholy, I wonder where that faraway
    frontier is,
And who will I rely on to deliver the traveler's
    clothes to my dear.

花信過容易。君何竟遠離。

恨無比翼兩相飛。獨抱香衾眠不寐

暗自悲。寒風透幕至。

恨望遠陽何處是。憑誰代妾寄征衣

JSGJ I.27b

    * "To have wings and fly side by side" alludes to the
lovers' closeness. It originates from *Erya*, an ancient
reference classic, and its romantic reference was popu-
larized in the Tang dynasty by poet Bo Juyi (772–846)
in his poetic rendition of the romance between Emperor
Xuanzong (reign years 713–55) and his consort Yang
Guifei.

61   I have sewn a fox-fur coat; it's ready to be sent.
      I look for someone to deliver it for me.
      The road to the frontier city is distant, beyond
         the vast horizon;
      Can somebody do me a favor, and take it to my
         husband?
      I've prepared it well.
      How can Husband get it?
      If there are trains as in the West,*
      I will be spared the terrible hassle of sending it by
         mail.

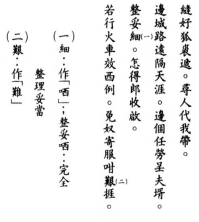

JSGJ I.52b

* "West" refers to the United States.

62 I wish to send traveler's clothes
To my husband somewhere outside.*
Is there a courier going to that end of the sky?
I hope it will reach Husband in time.
Humbly I bow;
On whom can I rely?
On the frontier, most fearsome are the strong
    winds and snows.
Sorrowful are those who endure the blizzards in
    thin clothes.

欲把征袍遞。良人在亞西。
有何驛使到天涯。願得應時呈夫壻。
頓首拜。邊個(一)能藉賴。
塞外最愁霜雪大。可憐衫少受風凄。

(一)邊個：誰人

JSGJ I.52b

* "Outside" could also be rendered as "Sierra." The
Chinese characters *a-sai* in this line might be a phonetic
reversal for rhyming purposes.

63   The young, rouge-faced woman cherishes her husband
    And fears most a separation: one here, the other there.
    My dearest love, why must you make a living in a
        foreign land?
    Besieged by sorrow, our youthful years are totally
        wasted.
    O, be on your guard:
    Don't be corrupted by vices.
    As an old saying goes: So many young men wander
        all over the world,
    Drifting around, forgetting the poor wife of husk
        at home.*

古語江湖多子弟。飄身忘却糟糠妻。

君何異地作生涯。兩悮青春愁莫解。

須緊戒。切莫邪行歪。

紅顏愛夫壻。最怕各東西。

JSGJ I.24a

*"Wife of husk": the wife who shares the suffering ("eats husk") with her husband before he becomes rich and prominent, as seen in the heroine Zhao Wuniang in *Pipa ji* (The Lute), a Yuan dynasty drama written by Gao Ming (fl. 1354).

64 Since you left for North America,
    You haven't thought of me for twenty long years.
    You've banished me to solitude and to my knitted
        brows.
    It's wrong for lovers to be separated in two places.
    O, you are bad!
    You don't feel a thing for your poor wife.
    You care only for your fun and games outside.
    And I must live with the fate of separation for the
        rest of my life!

自君遊北美。廿年不我記。
丢儂孤寡鎖雙眉。枉屈鴛鴦分兩地。
可惡汝。唔念諧連理。
在外風流顧一巳。虧奴半世守生離。

（一）
唔念：不想念

JSGJ II.39b

65 I am petrified by crazy nightmares
And Husband doesn't seem to care.
When we were married, as husband and wife,
    that year,
I thought he would treasure our conjugal tie.
Alas, who would have guessed:
He is a cruel wolf at heart.
He abandons me to solitude; my eyes are puffy
    from tears.
He lingers around Gold Mountain, and of me,
    he is hardly aware.

累奴成顛夢。婿作不關痛。
昔年與彼結雌雄。估佢夫妻情義重。
料唔中(一)。咁樣(二)狼心種。
丟妾形單哭眼腫。金山流戀(三)弗思儂。

（三）流戀：多作「留戀」
（二）咁樣：如此
（一）料唔中：料想不到

JSGJ II.39b

66　The betrothal presents were not yet prepared,
　　When husband-to-be sojourned in Gold Mountain.
　　It's been over sixteen years and he has not
　　　　returned.
　　He doesn't care about my grief and resentment
　　　　in the bedroom.
　　Quietly I sigh;
　　I am dying from all this thinking.
　　Why are you, my dear man, so nonchalant?
　　You waste my youth, as if it were nothing!

聘禮猶未辨。夫婿客金山。
年逾二八都唔還(一)。不理閨中人憾恨。
暗自嘆。條腸想到爛。
做乜(二)郎君心恁散。誤我青春作等閒。

（一）唔還：不回來
（二）做乜：為何

JSGJ II.40a

67   Right after we were wed, Husband, you set
          out on a journey.
      How was I to tell you how I felt?
      Wandering around a foreign country, when
          will you ever come home?
      You are wasting many joyous years of our
          precious youth.
      My spring heart has turned to ashes.
      Poverty does not allow me the luxury of a choice.
      But let it be known to all my sisters:
      Don't ever marry a young man going overseas!

于歸夫出外。有口實難開。
遨遊異國幾時回。負却風流經數載。
春心灰。家貧無可奈。
寄語同羣諸姊妹。出洋子弟勿相配。

JSGJ I.23b

68   The ship SS *Asia* has arrived.
      But Husband has not come home on it.
      Perhaps a delay, and he is on the SS *China*?
      Or maybe he's returning on the SS *Korea*.
      O, my mind is full of worries—
      I hope the news is not false.
      I am waiting: SS *Manchuria*, SS *Mongolia* . . .
      Finally the geese bring a word and everything
          turns blurry.*

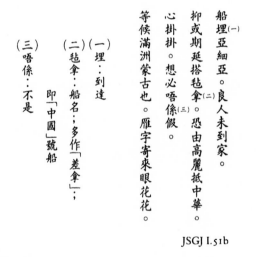

船埋亞細亞。良人未到家。
抑或期延搭毡拿⁽二⁾。恐由高麗抵中華。
心掛掛。想必係假⁽三⁾。
等候滿洲蒙古也。雁字寄來眼花花。

（一）埋：到達

（二）毡拿：船名；多作「差拿」；
        即「中國」號船

（三）唔係：不是

JSGJ I.51b

* "Geese," see song 28.

FOUR

Nostalgic Blues

Chinese men of letters have long written both poetry
and prose expressing the sojourner's nostalgia for home,
which is evoked by certain scenes and events. For
example, to the poets Li Bo (701–762) and Su Dongpo
(1036–1101) a full moon would automatically evoke
fond memories of home and family. A seasonal festival
made the sojourner's solitude more intense than ever,
as another poet, Wang Wei (701–761), lamented: "A
stranger alone in a strange place / All the more I think of
my family on a festive occasion." Later, vernacular
stories express both the happiness and the sorrow of a
man being away from home. His departure often led to
events, great and small, that would ultimately change
the individual as well as his family. For instance, in Feng
Menglong's "Pearl-Sewn Shirt," a man's family and the
life of his wife all went to ruin due to his prolonged
absence from home, as the wife succumbed to sexual
temptation. Being away from home has thus always
been a negative notion unless the sojourner will ulti-
mately return.

Home, or family, is always the most important part
of the Chinese societal structure. A Chinese family is
seen as a tree that grows with many branches extending
and outreaching; but every branch is physically part of
the tree. Once a branch is cut off from the tree trunk,
it cannot survive on its own. There is even a Chinese
proverb that says: "Fallen leaves return to the roots of
the tree." Along with that sense of belonging, of course,
comes the responsibility to safeguard the welfare of the
family. Each member must do his part to protect its
well-being, sacrificing his own personal comfort and
happiness, even his own life, for its preservation or
honor.

In Chinese perception, home is not just a man's castle.
It is also his ultimate "security blanket." Without it, he
would be at a loss during a time of crisis. With it, he
finds security among the stormy and unhappy events of
life. It provides its members with comfort and the true
sense of belonging. When Tao Qian (372?–427?), the
famous poet and prose writer, was totally frustrated by
life outside his home, he declared in indignation, "Why
don't I go home!"

This sense of returning home and belonging to the
family is central to the Chinese way of life. A person
cannot stay away from home throughout the year. Tra-
ditionally, he must rush home by the end of the year for
the grand family dinner on New Year's Eve, an occasion
no less significant than the family reunions at Thanks-
giving or Christmas in American society. Absence from
such an occasion occurs only if it is absolutely impossible
for the sojourner to make it home. Without the presence
of every family member, the reunion is not complete;
the happiness and joy for the New Year celebration
cannot be total. On such an occasion, members of the

family will then express their wishes for the sojourning member's early return.

In old China, no one leaves home if he can make a decent living in his native place. In fact, there were only three common situations in which a person would have to leave home. The first was the education expedition in preparation for the imperial examination, success in which would bring fame and honor to the family name. The second was exile, if a person had disgraced his family and was expelled from home as a punishment. The third was to seek a living outside, when a person could no longer survive on the means available at home. This last situation was, in fact, also a form of exile, one in which the sojourner took the burden and responsibility for the economic survival of the family. His triumphant return with economic success would be a vindication of having had to leave the family under such circumstances.

69 Though I've journeyed to the very ends of the earth,
I cannot forget my ancestral home.
The traveler, in the still of night, thinks of his
    family,
Tossing and turning, thoughts whirling, asleep,
    awake.
In dreams, my soul flies
Back to the village.
Fields and gardens seem barren and abandoned.
O, why didn't I go home? Why don't I go home?*

天涯遍作旅。難忘舊祖居。
遊人夜靜憶庭幃。展轉縈懷興復睡。
夢魂飛。返到故里處。
恍惚田園將荒廢。胡不歸兮胡不歸。

JSGJ I.11b

*The last two lines are borrowed from the prose
work "Homecoming" ("Gui qu lai xi ci") by the Jin
dynasty poet Tao Qian (372?–427?), who chose to re-
tire to a rustic life rather than humiliate himself as a
petty bureaucrat.

70   Since my departure in Hong Kong,
She and I are each in different places.
A long separation makes a person even more miserable.
How can one ever forget home, sweet home?
Stranded in a foreign country,
In dreams my soul encircles my village home.
Words to wife and children: don't worry, you won't
    have to wait too long.
Once I amass the gold, I will be on my way.

自從離香港。伊人各一方。
維桑與梓豈能忘。久別故園添苦況。
羈異邦。夢魂繞鄉黨。
寄語妻兒休掛望。黃金大有就回唐(一)。

（一）
唐：參看歌 #21

JSGJ II.41b

71 My loved one is far away.
Alone, by the railing, I look around aimlessly.
Many times, depressed by a bright, full moon, *
My body aches and twists with ninefold grief and
     pain.
A heart left hanging.
A deep love that cannot be severed.
Just how can we be reunited and share companionship
     again?
Spare me from sleeping with only a cold quilt and
     pillow.

怎得重逢同作伴。免吾寨宿枕衾寒。

掛胆肝。癡情難割斷。

幾回惱煞月圑圓。令我腸回(一)更九轉。

意中人隔遠。獨自倚欄看。

（一）
回：作「迴」

JSGJ I.43a

* "Full moon," see song 49.

72 Ever since I've arrived in Gold Mountain,
Not one day have I dared forget my family.
My mind is chaotic, like hemp fibers, with constant
thought of home;
Each meal is hard to swallow, because of sorrow.
My dear woman:
Don't ever think your husband has betrayed your
love.
It's hard enough to share my words with you in
dreams;
My soul is wandering, every night, my tongue
tightened.

自抵金山也。無日敢忘家。
心懷桑梓亂如蘇。每飯因愁難咽下。
亞卿呀。莫作夫情寡。
難夢與儂同講話。遊魂夜夜舌交加。

JSGJ I.12b

73   Living stranded under the Flowery Flag
Is like shouldering a heavy cangue.*
Never for one moment do I stop wishing to go
    back to China,
But the road is long and I cannot gallop away.
A heart left hanging—
Wife at home sends me these words:
You have been there across the ocean for a long,
    long time;
By all means, remember to come home soon.

羈居花旗下。身如荷重枷。
無時不欲返中華。可惜路遙難策馬。
心掛掛。室人曾有話(一)。
漫向外洋來久假。千祈記緊(二)早回家。

（一）千祈：千萬
（二）記緊：緊記

JSGJ I.12a

*"Cangue," see song 6.

74 My body aches; my heart pains me all the more.
Separation brings even more remorse.
Away at the edge of the horizon, everything seems
  remote;
In vain I long for my virtuous wife and my filial
  children.
For a husband and his wife—
The two sorrows share the same origin.
I endure sleepless nights thinking of home.
I wonder if anybody at home ever thinks of me?

身苦心猶苦。別離恨益多。

天涯遠隔事荒蕪。空憶賢妻和肖子。

婦與夫。兩愁同一路。

我記家人難夜度。未識家人記我無。

JSGJ I.12b

75 Who could have guessed the sojourn would last
     so long?
   Had I known, I wouldn't have come at all.
   Separated by many mountains and vast seas,
   I have forsaken wife and children to seek my fortune.
   Heart bleeds in pain.
   A sojourner thousands of miles from home.
   Time passes ever so quickly, but a reunion is so
     hard to come by;
   I just don't know when I can start my homebound
     journey.

誰估流咁奈。當初準唔來。
遠隔重山又重海。拋妻別子爲求財。
傷心哉。作客千里外。
光陰易過人難會。未知何日起程回。

（一）奈：作「耐」，長久

JSGJ I.12b

76 My friends, remember by all means:
Don't let yourselves be stranded in a foreign country.
Brows besieged by sorrow from frequent worries
   of home;
Thousands of miles of clouds and mountains further
   impede a gloomy stay.
Separation brings out misery.
Have your belongings always packed and ready.
A journey to America is only a search for wealth.
Return to the old country quickly, to avoid
   going astray.

勿困他邦地。同人要緊記。
家居復望鎖愁眉。暗滯雲山千萬里。
暌生悲。速整隨行裡(一)。
只為求財經旅美。早回故國免流離。

（一）裡：作「李」

JSGJ I.11b

77   The folks are still there, waiting by the gate.
     This traveler at the edge of the world has yet to
        return.
     It's hard to find the key to fortune.
     Thoughts of home are a grief multiplied hundredfold.
     I encountered an unusual disaster:
     The City fell victim to red flames. *
     When can I go back with songs of bountiful success,
     And spare the aged ones from becoming senile while
        they wait?

倚閭人尚在。天涯客未回。

此因利鎖實難開。思到家鄉愁百倍。

遇奇災。埠刦紅陽害。

幾得東旋歌捆載。免致年老望痴呆。

JSGJ I.15b

*The fire that destroyed San Francisco after the
1906 earthquake.

78 I bid farewell to Father and Mother.
Throughout the journey I worry and worry about
  them.
To get food, I have no choice but to hurry about;
My thoughts of them are all in a tangle, like hemp
  fibers.
Unable to return——
When will I again sit beside their knees?
An endless horizon severs family happiness.
As I long in vain for my parents, my eyes turn blurry.

別却爹和媽(一)。條腸一路掛。

爲口奔馳唔係假。庭幃牽念亂如蔴。

未歸家。幾時依膝下。

天涯間斷天倫也。陟岵徒勞眼望花。

（一）
唔係：參看歌#68

JSGJ I.14b

79   To chase after a pin-head gain,
I endured the separation from my mother.
Drifting on a voyage of thousands of miles,
I reached the Flowery Flag Nation to take my
    chances.
Sorrow is to be so far away from home.
I must burden Mother to send me clothes for my
    stay.
Unable to prepare the homebound whip, stranded
    in a foreign land,
O, when can I repay her kindness in raising me?

為逐蠅頭利。萱堂忍別離。

飄泊水程數萬里。精神冒險抵花旗⁽⁻⁾。

遠堪悲。征衣勞母寄。

未整歸鞭留異地。恩懷鞠育報何期。

（一）
花旗：參看歌#3

JSGJ I.14b

80 I've come, because of poverty, to a foreign country,
Cherishing the memory of my home state.
Again and again, I wish to go back, but am unable
    to set a date,
Tossing and turning, I am restless in a sojourner's
    bed.
Alone, sighing.
Thrice asleep, thrice awakened.
I pray tomorrow morning I can amass a hefty gain.
Then I'll buy a boat and return to Canton
    smiling in satisfaction.

因貧來異地。懷念我邦畿。
屢欲旋歸未有期。展轉旅床難入寐。
自歔欷。三眠又三起。
但願明朝得大利。買舟回粵笑微微。

JSGJ I.13a

81 Now that I've thought everything over:
   I am all confused.
   Needless to say I feel concern for my parents,
   I am also burdened with thoughts of my wife and
     children.
   Why so?
   'Cause I cannot make it home.
   I look around—north, south, east, west—and
   I don't know which direction is home.

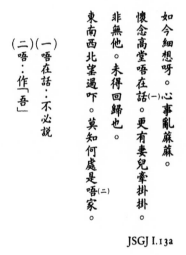

JSGJ I.13a

82 A long time away from home:
My family, an unavoidable concern.
In pain I left my parents to journey ten thousand
miles away.
Many times I wish to go back and be with them
again.
Autumns come and go.
I haven't succeeded in amassing silver and gold.
I pray Heaven will bless me:
Let me one day return in splendid clothes and spare
myself being thus detained.

離家日已久。難免內顧憂。

苦別雙親萬里遊。每欲旋歸同敘首。

秋過秋。黃白唔成就。

但願皇天常眷祐。他年衣錦免羈留。

JSGJ I.13a

83 Letters from home are frequent and urgent:
Urging me to return to China.
I hesitate: my purse is not full.
I am ashamed; I have no excuse for my fault.
But, how am I to explain it all?
So my homebound journey is postponed.
I'm only afraid my parents will be waiting with
ever-longing eyes.
O, why don't I just pack up for home now, while
there's still time?

家信催緊板，速我返唐山(一)。

私囊未愿進退難。自問多慚難以挽。

言不堪。歸期因此慢。

只恐高堂望穿眼。不如趁早把鄉還。

（一）
唐山∴參看歌
#21

JSGJ. I.12b

84 Often I dream of the moment I return to South
       China.
    When the dream ends, my eyes are in a daze.
    In dream after dream, I'm back in Sunning:*
    Wife, children, the village well—all in my dreams.
    O, let the dreams never end.
    Dream again, another wonderful dream.
    But dreams of my prolonged incarceration here
       set my heart aflame.
    Dream, dream—how I would like to dream of being
       home again!

JSGJ I.12a

*Sunning (Xinning) is the former name of Toisaan
(Taishan).

85　The world outside my village is vast, without a
　　　boundary in sight.
　　I'm cut off from my village by mountains and seas.
　　Away from my village, searching for gold and
　　　silver,
　　In melancholy, I long for the sight of the village
　　　gate tower.
　　I think of things back in the village.
　　Since leaving my village, I haven't returned.
　　Messages from the village are filled with ten
　　　million complaints.
　　Remembering my village, I wish to follow the
　　　geese home.*

外鄉無限恨。鄉里隔河山。

暌違鄉境覓金銀。惆悵鄉臺空望眼。

想鄉間。離鄉身未返(一)。

鄉音責我言千萬。迴憶鄉間逐雁還。

（一）
迴：作「回」

JSGJ I.11b

* "Geese," see songs 28 and 53.

86 The journey is thousands of miles of vast distance.
From afar, I remember my home garden.
My dear wife must be tossing and turning in her sleep,
    waiting for me.
O, how I wish my business will bring me fortune.
To South China, I would return:
My young son would stare at me by the door;
Brothers would meet, like geese after a long journey.
And, my parents would beam happily in the living
    room.

程途里數萬。遙憶故園間。
嬌情寐寐望子還。但愿生意銀多賺。
返唐山(一)。迎門稚子盻。
兄弟相逢如鴻雁。椿萱堂上笑開顏。

（一）唐山：參看歌 #21

JSGJ I.12a

87   Drifting all this way to seek some gain,
     I've forsaken my family for a long time.
     No need to linger in the Flowery Flag Nation,
     Pack up my belongings and go home!
     This is truly my wish:
     Leave this barbaric land on the earliest possible
          day.
     It can't be compared to the warmth of home;
     My heart cares only for the day of my return.

漂身來覓利。家人久拋棄。
何須依戀在花旗⁽⁻⁾。收拾行裝旋故里。
儂所冀。早離番邦地。
桑梓殷情無可比。一心懷念轉歸期。

（一）
花旗：參看歌#3

JSGJ I.12b

88　Held stranded many years in a travelers' lodge,
The sojourner harbors a restless mind.
With prolonged anxiety, I remember the fields and
　　gardens back at home:
A lingering emotion spans the two continents, and
　　my heart is nearly broken.
Mind and soul are full of worry.
An empty purse always depresses me.
Suddenly, in a dream, I'm back in the village;
But alas, my body still remains in the Golden
　　Gate!

多年羈旅館。遊子志難安。
悠悠我念故田園。兩地情牽腸欲斷。
掛心肝⁽一⁾。囊空常抱悶。
徒然夢裡回鄉轉。誰知身尚在金門。

（一）掛心肝：掛在心頭

JSGJ II.40b

89 A sojourn in Canada:
A duckweed's trace, my stay uncertain.*
Looking back, home is way beyond the horizon;
Ambitions are unfulfilled, sorrows unresolved.
In debt, up to my neck.
I wonder if prosperity ever comes after extreme
    misfortune.
I wish to raise the homebound whip, but with an
    empty purse—
Cloudy mountains seem so distant; my bosom aches
    with emotion.

旅居加拿大。萍踪靡定棲。
故園回首隔天涯。壯志莫伸愁莫解。
周身(一)債。難逢否極泰。
欲整歸鞭囊若洗。雲山沙沙感予懷。

（一）周身：滿身

JSGJ II.41a

*"A duckweed's trace" alludes to a person's living
in a transient state.

90   Since I came to San Francisco,
     Father and Mother are with me in dreams.
     No longer can I attend to them piously morning and
        evening;
     Family needs force me to become a wanderer.
     Wounded with silent grief,
     A traveler stranded on this American sojourn.
     Each festival arouses my feelings of home.
     For parents' love and health, a son must show his
        concern.

佳節每逢情觸起。親心善體是為兒。

儿杖晨昏難奉侍。無何家計迫飄離。

暗傷悲。客行羈歐美。

自抵三藩市。嚴慈夢寐依。

JSGJ I.15a

91   This wanderer left home long ago.
      Who is taking care of the ancestors' graves?
      When Cold Food Day comes each year, I alone am
         in tears.*
      Unwilling to fawn upon the rich, I maintain
         myself in poverty.
      Stranded on the American continent,
      How can I be with my family again?
      I wish to set sail for home, but my fortune is
         not yet made.
      My parents' kindness, my wife's faith—I grieve
         I might not be able to repay them.

欲買歸舟財未就。親恩妻義恨難酬。
困美洲。家人奚聚首。
每逢寒食淚偷流。媚富不甘貧自守。
遊子離鄉久。祖墓情誰修。

JSGJ II.55b

   *Cold Food Day is the day before the Qing Ming
festival (Pure-Bright Day, usually around April 5 or
April 6), the day to pay respects and offer sacrifices
to the deceased of the family. No cooking with fire
is done on Cold Food Day.

92 Months and years, like a current, flow along.
    Counting on my fingers, I realize it's now the middle
        of the eighth month. *
    Tonight is marvelous, moonlight at the doorsteps;
    The moon, crystal-clear, so round and full.
    I view the moon.
    But seeing the moon arouses my sorrow.
    The moon makes me long for home, so far away.
    Leaning by the rail before the full, round moon,
        all in vain.

因月思鄉鄉隔遠。倚欄空帳月華圓。

對月觀。見月生愁想。

斯宵佳景月臨門。皎皎月輪分外滿。

歲月如流轉。屈指八月半。

JSGJ I.49a

*Referring to the "Mid-autumn Festival," cele-
brated on the fifteenth day of the eighth lunar month.
A full moon symbolizes a union, especially of families
or lovers.

93 Although it's a long time since I came to the West,
My homeland is truly my heartfelt concern.
Her mountains and passes, ten thousand miles away,
    beyond the mist and fog;
She is now a bean split, a melon carved—O, what
    a horror!*
Fellow countrymen:
Please end all partisan disputes!
A united republic of north and south would be
    so grand;
How can you tolerate civil strife and chaos in China?

南北共和如此雅。那堪內訌亂中華。

同胞呀。消融黨界罷。

關山萬里隔烟霞。豆剖瓜分眞係怕。

西來雖久假。祖國實心掛。

JSGJ II.44a

＊"Bean split" is an allusion to internal disputes;
"melon carved" refers to annexation by outsiders.
These are specific references to the political turmoil at
the founding of the Republic of China in 1911.

FIVE

Rhapsodies on Gold

The collapse of the Taiping Revolt in 1864 and then the failure of the Chinese intellectuals' Hundred Day Reform in 1898 brought a number of Chinese political exiles to the United States for refuge. However, what brought the great majority of early Chinese immigrants to America was the most basic human need, economic survival. Their Pearl River delta homeland, the Cantonese "rice bowl," had been devastated by natural disasters and by social unrest brought on by both the foreign imperialism of the British and French and regional ethnic conflicts between Cantonese natives and Hakka settlers. The result was famine and starvation, which forced the able bodied to leave home in order to survive. And, since the delta region was the gateway for foreign trade and international exchange, why not go abroad? Labor recruitment and commercial opportunities in the United States offered a strong new attraction. Thus, the Cantonese, not unlike other newcomers to the United States in the latter half of the nineteenth century, were drawn to the United States as a land of plenty in which to realize their dreams of wealth. They, too, heard the call: "Go West, young man!"

The Chinese contingent of new arrivals came to California hoping above all for financial success. Decades later, however, many of them no longer harbored illusions of becoming rich through hard work. Nor did they still patiently hope for the equal opportunity to strike it rich in the land of equal opportunity. Still, they could not just pack up and return home empty-handed, for to do so would be to admit failure and to declare that the journey to America had been made in vain.

Hard-luck American reality, thus, led many of these men to fanastic wishes of wealth. In the wild West, there were ample chances to take a lucky shot at a game of chance. For those who were down and out, the game of chance seemed to represent a truly "equal," though remote, opportunity to materialize the dream of wealth. After all, no one had come to work in California, the Gold Mountain, without having hopes of becoming rich. Hard work might, eventually, be rewarded; but a sudden stroke of luck could at once alter a person's improverished lot. Perhaps this rationale explains the widespread indulgence in gambling in the West. It was engaged in not only by the Chinese but also by hard-working laborers, merchants, and fortune-seekers of every ethnic background. To all of them, luck and the game of chance appeared to be a yellow brick road to financial success.

The Chinese immigrants were not bashful about the objective of their journey across the Pacific Ocean. They freely expressed their preference for wealth, as we see in these poems. On festive occasions such as Chinese New

Year, they would greet each other with good wishes not just for a happy new year, but for a new opportunity to become rich and to improve their lot in America. They would toast not only the arrival of the new year but also their aspiration for wealth and the coming of financial success, so that their hardship stay could soon end and they could return home with a true sense of accomplishment—to make the homebound trip with suitcases full of gold and money.

94 The very moment when the Wealth Star favors me,
　Wealth will come naturally.
　Wealth will arrive without sweat and toil;
　Wealth will bring more wealth through its wide
　　and open road.
　The air of wealth will soar.
　Wealth will bring me recognition.
　A man of wealth is famous, a generous spender;
　Wealth will make a rich tycoon out of this
　　poverty-sticken soul.

財星一朝好。財白自然到。

財來不必苦勤勞。財生財有亨通道。

財氣高。財發人識我。

財主揚名稱闊佬(一)。財成窮漢變富豪。

（一）
闊佬：花錢很多的人

JSGJ I.7b

95 A son, or money—which is more precious?
    On top, of course, is money.
    Without money, liberty and rights are beyond your
    means.
    Parents take care of a son, but money takes care of
    your skin.
    Money is everything.
    What's more convenient than having money on a
    spending spree?
    A son wastes his father's money; nothing unusual
    about that indeed.
    But a father can only drool in vain over his son's
    money!

兒錢究孰善。本係錢為先。
無錢難講自由權。膝下顧丁錢顧面。
錢高見。勝使錢方便。
子費父錢誠弗鮮。子錢父怕枉垂涎。

（一）使錢：用錢，花錢

JSGJ I.46a

96   Sons and grandsons are dearest to one's heart.
      Yet money is a foundation of life.
      A hundred thousand dollars in a money belt
         will enable you to survive;
      Even the filiality of a crow is no comparison.*
      Remember, by all means:
      Profits and privileges are all in your possession.
      A son may be illustrious and outstanding,
      But you and your money should never have a
         separation!

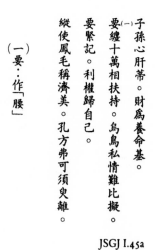

子孫心肝蒂。財爲養命基。
要⁽一⁾纏十萬相扶持。烏鳥私情難比擬。
要緊記。利權歸自己。
縱使鳳毛稱濟美。孔方弗可須臾離。

（一）要：作「腰」

JSGJ I.45a

*In Chinese legend, the crow is a bird of filial piety.

97 The mournful sight of dreaded autumn, a sudden
    fright:
   Time flies in the blinking of an eye.
   Money is no casual matter;
   As the old saying goes: beware of future falls.
   In no time—
   Poverty will drive you up the wall.
   What comfort to store grain and avoid hunger in
    later years
   And not to live on only one meal a day.

頓覺驚秋恨。轉瞬幾十眼。
青蚨莫作當為閒。古語有云顧後患。
怎陣間。無錢就撞板 (一)。
積穀防飢慰景晚。勿俾 (二) 這時捱單餐。

(一) 撞板：碰壁
(二) 勿俾：不要讓

98   All of a sudden, my luck is piping hot:
I've found treasures, filled in several pots.
In no time I've become a young man of wealth;
I turn around, and I'm no longer a part of that
    miserable lot.
I am a millionaire—
Right now I can open a bank.
What can be more delightful than having unexpected
    wealth?
I will buy land, build a house, and get myself a
    concubine.

霎時財氣旺。撿得寶數缸。

忽然變作富家郎。回首身價唔同講。

幾十方。即刻開銀庄。

意外發來心更爽(一)。置田納妾起樓房。

（一）
爽：痛快

JSGJ I.6a

99 Those were the days of extreme hardship and pain.
    And of suffering much misery.
    Suddenly, the Spirit of Money graces my thatched
       hut,
    Carrying greenbacks and flying in through the
       window.
    I look around:
    It's all gold and silver, I've lost count.
    In one blink I've become a rich young man.
    From now on I am no longer a poor soul living
       in desperation!

昔時極艱苦。捱得凄涼多。
忽然銀精到茅廬。竟擁青蚨飛入戶。
回頭顧。黃白計無數。
瞬息變爲富家子。從今唔使做窮徒。

（一）
唔使：參看歌 #32

JSGJ I.7b

100　At the moment, I hardly have enough grub to
　　　eat.
　　But I won't take it as fate, my final destiny.
　　I don't believe I will live like this till my hair
　　　turns white;
　　It's only the low ebb in my life.
　　When luck strikes,
　　With the whole world behind me,
　　I will be rich in a few years' turn.
　　And then, I will buy property and build a
　　　Western mansion.

目下難餬口。造化睇未透⁽一⁾。

唔信⁽二⁾這樣到白頭。祇因眼前命不偶。

運氣湊。世界還在後。

轉過幾年富且厚。恁時置業起洋樓。

（一）
睇透：看透

（二）
唔信：不相信

JSGJ II.44a

101 Since rushing to this foreign place,
    I have been down and out in the Flowery Flag
        Nation.
    I figure it's been more than thirty years—
    My plans are unrealized; I am still waiting for
        that magic moment.
    At last, my wishes are granted:
    The God of Wealth follows me from behind.
    My purse stuffed full of foreign dollars;
    I'll set a date and make ready the homebound whip.

自從奔異地。落拓在花旗(一)。
屈指算來年卅幾。求謀未遂待乘時。
今得志。財神跟住尾(二)。
洋蚨富足荷包裡。整定歸鞭有日期。

（一）花旗：參看歌#3
（二）跟在尾：跟隨在後面

JSGJ II.13a

102 In a sojourn in San Francisco,
Luck and wealth grace me as spring arrives.
With trunks full of yellow eagles, it's time to
head home;*
Right away my boat ticket and visa are prepared
and ready.
O, truly wonderful—
I bid farewell to all my good friends.
I am returning home with purses and bags stuffed
full.
Soon, I will see my parents' brows beaming with
joy.

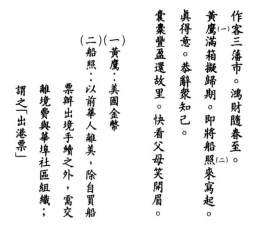

作客三藩市。鴻財隨春至。
黃鷹(一)滿箱擬歸期。即將船照(二)來寫起。
眞得意。恭辭衆知己。
囊橐豐盈還故里。快看父母笑開眉。

（二）（一）
船照黃鷹
：：
以美
前國
華金
人幣
離
美
，
除
自
買
船
票辦出境手續之外，需交
離境費與華埠社區組織；
謂之「出港票」

JSGJ I.53b

*"Yellow eagles"—a term used by the Chinese in
America for U.S. gold coins.

103 Our idle talk often runs to wealth and
nobility.
Shouting and resounding, reaching far and
near.
My head turns—my, what silver and gold!
Getting rich is indeed wonderful.
I'll change all my clothes.
Today I'll be different from before.
At once I will return to my village home by
boat;
I am young, but I'll be called an expert in
business circles.

富貴隨口講。喊響數十方。
回頭正是白兼黃。發達起來眞係爽（一）。
改過裝。今時不比往。
即刻買舟還梓桑。縱然大叔稱在行。

（一）爽：參看歌
#98

JSGJ I.7a

104 At a moment of tremendous opportunity,
They all come—happiness, prosperity, longevity,
and peace.
Treasures from mother nature are rewards for one's
good deeds;
Once wealth and nobility arrive, the success story is
complete.
With fast-expanding wealth,
I'll turn around and go back to Canton by sea.
No need to wait for luck in the pick-six exacta;
I'll just take nature's endless bounty as it flows.

雲時好機會。福祿壽泰來。

天然獲寶由博愛。倏得富貴全滿載。

快發財。回頭歸粵海。

六連勝彩何須待。永利源來盡收埋。

JSGJ I. 7b

105 I am red hot under the Wealth Star.
In no time I have made a million.
My savings, kept in a vault, are all yellow
gold.
O, far away, my wife and children must be
waiting for me anxiously.
I prepare the traveling clothes.
I'll set out within a few days by boat.
With favorable winds, I will reach Hong Kong
safe and sound;
Everyone will rush out to greet this wealthy
sojourner coming home.

財星真係旺。驟然幾十方。

庫中財蓄鑕全黃。遙想妻孥時盼望。

束行裝。近日催舟往。

風順一帆安抵港。爭看富客歸家堂。

JSGJ I. 53a

106 The God of Wealth showers me with blessings.
The Ghost of Poverty goes a far distance away.
Right away I hit it big, with purses stuffed
full;
I even find hidden treasures while taking a
stroll.
I will buy a farm.
The present can't compare with the past.
Truly delightful is fortune coming from every
direction.
I'll hurry back to South China, with a hundred
thousand dollars secured around my waist.

財神將當旺。窮鬼遠他方。
即時發達就豐裘。移步唔難與寶藏(一)。
置田庄。今時不比往。
左右逢源眞係爽(二)。腰纏十萬即回唐。

（一）
唔難：不困難

（二）
爽：參看歌 #98

JSGJ I.6b

107 In the beginning I was just a poor soul.
Suddenly, I am rich and noble.
It's not an illusion to have a splendid mansion
 or a luxurious home;
I think fate must be the cause of my past ill
 fortune.
With a push from luck,
Gold and silver will fill my lot.
As life changes for the better, wealth accumulates in
 heaps;
Clothed in silk, with a hundred thousand dollars
 wrapped around my waist, I'll return in triumph.

當初窮過鬼(一)。霎時富且貴。
唔難屋潤又家肥。回憶囊空因命水(二)。
運氣催。黃白從心遂。
否極泰來財積聚。腰纏十萬錦衣歸。

(二)(一)
命窮
水過
：鬼
命：
運比
　窮
　鬼
　還
　差

JSGJ I.6b

108 It's a summerlike first month of the new year.
Ten thousand houses are decorated with New
    Year scrolls.
In a foreign country, we celebrate the joyous
    festival in springtime clothes;
We greet each other by the door, with auspicious
    sayings:
May you claim a mine full of gold.
May wealth soothe your soul.
Hosts and guests, so gaily, raise the jade winecups,
Sipping the spring wine, toasting merrily the
    swift, rosy clouds.

寅建時行夏。桃符貼萬家。

異鄉春服鬧繁華。恭喜登門講好話。

拉金砂。發財稱心也。

賓主聯歡酬玉罡。屠蘇酒酌醉流霞。

JSGJ I.33a

109 All the auspicious greetings, I deeply appreciate.
A prominent future will follow the New Year's Day.
Brows beam with joy at the wonderful moment of
an approaching spring,
I sincerely wish good luck and peace to fellow
Chinese sojourners in America.
With a soaring spirit,
I present you a greeting card in return.
New Year gatherings are filled with immeasurable
gaiety;
When we are all rich enough, let's set an early
date for home.

多蒙齊恭喜。元旦大有機。
臨春佳景樂揚眉。祝福華僑安旅美。
高志氣。吉東復呈汝。
歲首相逢歡莫比。同人富足早歸期。

JSGJ I. 33b

110 New Year's Day starts a new calendar year.
The scent of spice fills the air beyond the front
door.
Pouring cups of spring wine, toasting up to our
brows,
Everywhere, we Chinese sojourners greet each other
with auspicious sayings.
In joyous laughter,
We wish good luck to others, and to ourselves:
May this year be prosperous for all walks of life;
So that, clothed in silk, we can together bid the
Flowery Flag farewell.

元旦更鳳紀。臨門盡椒氣。
高斟春酒以介眉。四處華僑言恭喜。
笑嬉嬉。祝人兼祝己。
今歲營謀皆順利。一齊衣錦別花旗。

JSGJ I.32b

111 Those were the days, the penniless days.
 Prosperity comes after extreme misfortune.
 As soon as I sprint over to the other side, I will
   be rich for sure;
 It's no bother at all to move my feet to become
   a wealthy fellow.
 When good luck reigns,
 Heaven will shower me with many blessings.
 In a game of chance, I instantly win the daily
   double.
 Without any effort, I have a hundred thousand
   dollars secured around my waist.

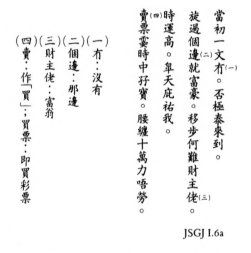

當初一文冇⁽一⁾。否極泰來到。
旋過個邊⁽二⁾就富豪。移步何難財主佬⁽三⁾。
⁽四⁾時運高。皁天庇祐我。
賣票雲時中孖寶。腰纏十萬力唔勞。

（一）冇∶沒有
（二）個邊∶那邊
（三）財主佬∶富翁
（四）賣∶作「買」∶買票∶即買彩票

JSGJ I.6a

112 Living in adversity, as always,
Then things suddenly come my way.
Unexpected wealth falls into my hands through
the square city;*
I will buy a boat and return to my village
right away.
Everything will be smooth.
Friends and relatives will come to wish me
well.
I will buy ten thousand acres of land and build
a mansion.
With a luxurious house, I can show off my rich
and prosperous family.

一向當逆景。忽然遂心稱。
橫財就手四方城。即刻(一)買舟回鄉井。
事事勝。親朋來相請。
立宅置田千萬頃。家肥屋潤顯門廷。

(一)
即刻：立刻

JSGJ II.12b

* "Square city" is a Cantonese idiom for a game of mahjong.

113 You need not come haunting me,
Accusing me of not returning home.
A thousand dollars is petty cash; but shoud I hit
the jackpot thrice:
It will explode into millions just like that,
believe me!
Won't that be great?
I will hurry and make the sailing date for China.
I will go first class, with yellow eagles stuffed
in several suitcases.*
I will return home, act like a big shot, and live
in extravagance.

汝唔駛嚟話(一)(二)。咕我唔歸家。
千員寮番中三吓。個陣發成千萬架(三)。
得意呀。船期赶差拿。
幾箱黃鷹(四)頭位卡(五)。還鄉充派(六)開繁華。

(六)派：作「派」；充派：誇張排場

(五)頭位卡：頭等艙

(四)黃鷹：參看歌#102

(三)架：粵方言語氣强調作用之尾詞

(二)嚟話：如此説

(一)唔駛：不必；參看歌#32

JSGJ. I.53b

*"Yellow eagle," see song 102.

114 In just a few hands, I wipe out the house for good.
Immediately I pack my suitcases for the journey.
Bags and trunks, all full of shiny yellow coins,
I rush aboard the liner to return to Hong Kong.
I have first-class accommodations,
In the company of nobles and officials.
Truly delightful is a homecoming in wealth and
triumph;
I will buy land, take a concubine, and build a
mansion.

幾場中起廠⁽一⁾。即刻整行裝。

箱盈篋滿鏹全黃。過赶船期返香港。

搭頭艙。官宦同來往。

富足榮旋真係爽⁽三⁾。置田立妾起樓房。

（一）廠：即「票廠」，指經營彩票（白鴿票，
　　　字花）的架步

（二）即刻：參看歌 #112

（三）爽：參看歌 #98

JSGJ I.53b

115 Lucky for me, fate took a turn.
I have one hundred thousand in cash wrapped
around my waist.
I packed my clothes, and took the SS *China*;
Fed with sumptuous feasts, greeted humbly, and
accorded courtesy.
I am pleased with myself.
Soon I'll make friends during the journey.
In no time, we will pass Japan, via Honolulu;
With a favorable wind, we will reach Hong Kong
safe and sound.

辛得時運轉。腰纏十萬貫。

束裝就搭差拿船。盛饌躬逢情有欵。

暗自歡。即時來約伴。

不日檀山經日本。順風到港祝平安。

JSGJ I.53b

116 I regret leaving home so long ago.
I want to return, but I don't have a penny.
How lucky it would be to realize my wishes in my
    job and a game of chance:
Money will come, piling as high as a mountain.
Then I will quickly retire.
With cashier's checks stuffed inside my sleeves,
Friends and relatives all feasting me farewell,
In no time I will be a rich man in Asia.

自恨離家久。思歸文無有。

何幸正偏(一)皆就手。資財厚蓄似山邱。

身速抽。赤紙(二)籠滿袖。

親朋爭做餞行酒。轉眼富翁到亞洲。

（一）
正偏：正當職業及「偏門」
　　　（即賭博）生活

（二）
赤紙：支票；亦音譯作「昃紙」

JSGJ I.53a

117   I've returned to Hong Kong from America,
With one hundred thousand dollars securely
    wrapped around my waist.
My hair is long, my face dirty, like a beggar;
My denim mule clothes are like a net, all torn and
    tattered.*
I went up to King Fong Restaurant.
The maître d'hôtel ignored me.
Then a gentleman in a long gown came over and sized
    me up;
After tea and tobacco, they even offered me betel nuts.

由美返香港。腰纏十萬方。

髮長面垢似花郎(一)。穿件縣布如爛網。

上瓊芳。公廨問唔講(二)。

長衫客來着眼望。茶煙奉罷又檳榔。

(一)花：作「化」，化郎：叫化子

(二)唔講：不説話

JSGJ I.10a

*"Mule clothes" refers to the workingman's garb made famous by the mule-and-spade label of the Levi Strauss Company.

Songs of Western Influence
and the American-borns

For early Chinese immigrants, immigration to the United States ultimately meant a challenging new life. They had to leave something behind, give up something old, and accept many new things. It was not possible for them to continue to live a pre-immigration existence, no matter how they tried. When time and place change, people naturally change accordingly as a matter of evolution and adaptation.

Although the early immigrants established what they called the "Canton of the West," Chinatown was never the Canton of China. Non-Chinese visitors there found that for all its exotic Asian flavor, there was a familiar American accent to almost everything in Chinatown. Chinese visitors to Chinatown perceived it as an American invention, camouflaged in quasi-Chinese colors. Familiar yet different, Chinatown was authentic to neither culture, because Chinatown was (and is) an American ethnic community, the home of Chinese immigrants, not just a replica of some city in China. As a community, it has made numerous adjustments in its way of life and cultural perceptions, and has emerged with its own unique identity, and its residents, with their own perspective on matters surrounding them.

The rhymes in this chapter illustrate the early Chinese immigrants' responses to and interpretations of life in their new home. They were eager to experiment with the new world and to re-evaluate the old one. The sensibility and perspective on life that emerged do not represent a melting pot mentality—a mere combination of the old and new. Instead, theirs was the product of a continuous fusion of the East and West—a brand-new, independent viewpoint based on the experiences gained from living in America among a variety of ethnic groups. These rhymes address the many cross-cultural matters that challenged them as immigrants and reveal a characteristic Chinatown perspective on the issues. Their views on personal wealth, family lineage responsibilities, and other ethical obligations are a re-examination of their own traditional cultural heritage in the light of living in a new environment, punctuated with a new priority of values. Their opinions regarding the issues of equal rights for women and freedom of love and marriage show a recognition of the issues from both sides. They were able to see what they considered as flaws in both cultures' outlooks. More importantly, their viewpoints on the issue of Westernization dramatized the significance of the issue of identity to the Chinatown community. Chinese Americans recognized the importance of accepting the new, because it was their newly acquired identity. At the same time, they also wanted to balance the change by holding on to the old values they brought with them from China.

Many immigrants were alarmed and disheartened, however, when they witnessed the extremes of the younger generation's new pattern of behavior. Their criticism of the younger generation was not so much a display of anti-Western sentiment as dismay that the younger generation was so influenced by what they perceived as vices of the American culture. To the immigrant generation, these vices represented the ignorant, uncivilized side of the Western lifestyle. Ignorance and incivility were the causes of numerous discriminatory practices in America which had victimized them as immigrants. Seeing such vices in the younger generation, the immigrants voiced their disapproval by recalling the values of the old country.

118 Since I left South China,
I have changed my clothes to the Western style.
I seek praise for being neat and fashionable
Though I have yet to speak with an American
tongue.
Smart in appearance—
Who dares to call me an ignorant fool?
A loose gown with wide sleeves brings only
scurrilous remarks
And it gets you nowhere, even if you are modern
in education.

自從離兩廣。服色轉西裝。
爭誇齊整兼在行。花語雖然未嚕講[二]。
週身光[三]。誰敢話雯憨[四]。
闊袖長袍招誹謗。縱深新學亦收庄[五]。

（一）花語：花旗話，即英語
（二）未嚕：還不會
（三）光：光鮮
（四）雯憨：土氣傻瓜
（五）收庄：不能作主持

JSGJ I.11a

119 Before your social status is revealed,
You are first judged by the brilliance of your
clothes.
No need to boast about whatever talents you might
have—
Nowadays, in any situation, the exterior is what
counts the most.
My fellow countrymen:
One day we might celebrate a happy occasion.
But if you don't have something presentable to cover
your birthday suit,
Who will choose you to propose a toast in front of
everyone?

未識身貴賤。首辦服媸妍。
遑論胸中何本領。皮相如今到處然。
同鄉井。或時有喜慶。
若無楚楚來蓋面。飲酒誰推汝在前。

JSGJ I.11a

120   With a mere glance at the fur coat,
      Courtesy and hospitality are accorded in earnest,
      Regardless of one's vulgarity or sophistication;
      So what if you are learned and civil?
      Who is to know?
      A blue garb is simply despicable.
      So, even if you face poverty and an empty rice bowl,
      You must by all means put up a front with a few
         items of smart apparel.

睇下副皮鼠。接待禮頻施。

不分庸與濁清奇。縱使談書和識理

有誰知。藍褸看唔起⁽²⁾。

寧可抵窮無米煮。要冲幾件光棍皮⁽⁴⁾。

（一）睇下：放眼一看

（二）看唔起：看不起

（三）冲：作「充」；參看歌 #113

（四）光棍皮：光鮮外表（衣服）

121 Spring returns to the continent.
Soothing is the misty scenery.
Flowers by the hundreds in red, by the thousands in
purple, all noble and rich;
Everywhere, towers and terraces, all decorated with
brilliant lanterns.*
It's a delight to the heart.
I sightsee in the Golden City,†
Eyes darting around, spirit dashing about, what
genuine joy—
Entertaining myself, I have forgotten about going
home.

春回大陸地。烟景堪人宜。
萬紫千紅花富貴。處處樓臺燈色美。
爽心機。看遍金城裡。
游目騁懷眞趣味。風光娛我却忘歸。

(一)金城‥金門城，即舊金山

JSGJ 1.32a

*The Lantern Festival is the fifteenth day of the first
lunar month; it concludes the Lunar New Year Festival.
†"Golden City" is short for Golden Gate City, i.e.,
San Francisco.

122 I have a bellyful of grudges and frustrations.
Where can I go to unwind?
I have heard about the many scenic spots in the park;
Leisurely, I stroll along the path that lies before me
Looking around.
Indeed this makes me forget all my troubles.
They say running amidst flowers is not a proper
 thing to do;
But you can get rid of your worries only by
 having fun.

牢騷裝滿肚。何處可消磨。

聞道園林景色多。盡向前途聊散步。

首四顧。能忘心事苦。

漫謂尋芳非正務。釋憂須在樂中圖。

JSGJ II.16a

123 A cool breeze, a warm day,
　　A leisurely walk around the New Garden.*
　　Willows green, peaches red, all are marvelous
　　　　sights;
　　I don't mind the fragrant paths leading a
　　　　distance away.
　　All the more delighted,
　　I wander along, to the east, to the west.
　　Each blade of grass and every blooming flower
　　　　can cheer a troubled mind.
　　O, why not take it easy and enjoy everything all
　　　　over again?

臨風和日暖。舉履步新園⁽一⁾。

柳綠桃紅色好觀。逐漸不嫌芳徑遠。

益喜歡。東隨西蕩轉。

草草花花能解悶。無妨輪復子⁽二⁾細看。

（一）新園：新公園，即金門公園

（二）子：作「仔」

JSGJ I.31a

*"New Garden"—a term for Golden Gate Park
used by the Chinese in San Francisco during the 1900s.

124   School lets out for the summer.
      No need to go home right away.
      Bustling are the parks and museums;
      So, hurry and rent a bicycle*
      Just to ride around.
      Start pedaling, roll down the streets!
      It's soothing and pleasing to the soul, a truly
          dashing experience.
      But my companions tease me about what a big
          show-off I am.

學堂放暑假。未可遠回家。
公園物院幾繁華。快倩自由車一架。
即管駕。動機隨街下。
淑性陶情眞消灑。同人漫笑我爲沙⁽一⁾。

（一）沙：沙塵；炫耀自己

JSGJ II.16b

*The bicycle is called a "foot-pedaled free vehicle" (*geukdaap jiyauche*) and the automobile, "engine-propelled free vehicle" (*geidung jiyauche*). Since the original gives simply *jiyauche*, it could be either a bicycle or an automobile. The subjects here are students, so bicycle appears to be a more suitable rendition.

125 A son is not totally dependable,
The toil of raising him is all but futile.
Blood kin becoming strangers in the streets
  is not at all a strange sight;
That's the practice, especially in Europe and
  America.
Each one flies his own way.
Liberty is not concerned with filial piety.
You should save enough for later while you're
  still able;
Spare yourself from suffering cold and hunger
  when you are old.

男兒不足恃。劬勞膜外置。

途人骨肉不為奇。風氣何況尤歐美。

各自飛。自由忘孝義。

當逞及時籌私己。免至臨老抵寒飢。

JSGJ 1.45b

126 American ways are very extreme.
   This worn writing brush cannot reveal them
      all.
   Just let me show you one ridiculous example
      in brief,
   And I must warn you, gentlemen, before you
      die of shock from hearing this news:
   There was a lawless shrew—
   She bullied and humiliated her inept husband;
   She divorced him, seized and sold the family
      property;
   Then, she openly found and married another man!

歐美風俗屬。禿筆寫唔細(一)。

舉彼荒唐事略提。恐令男界聞驚斃。

不法妻。欺凌愚拙婿。

分拆還佔家產賣。公然另擇別郎締。

（一）細：作「唿」；唔唿：不完

JSGJ II.30a

127 The emancipated women are the most shameful;
Their mouths are filled with foreign speech.
They loiter around with men day and night,
  everywhere,
Showing no respect for the husbands they married.
They are out of control.
How can a decent man challenge such a woman?
He resorts to remonstrating with kind and wise
  words;
Pity no shrews can appreciate such kind intent.

醜極自由女。滿口泰西語。

日夜同人[一]遊各處。不看良人在眼內。

唔受拘[二]。純夫難抗拒。

惟有善言來教佢。惜乎潑婦不知趣。

（一）同人：跟別人

（二）唔受拘：不受約束

JSGJ I.37b

128 Morality is despised: too stiff and confining.
The charming girl is spoiled beyond control.
She soars high, wanting to be equal to man,
Casting away chastity, treating propriety with
contempt.
If two hearts are in agreement,
She will consent to marry a man.
She claims to be civilized, following the Western
ways.
Well, we may as well forget about eating the roasted
pig.*

謬託文明遵西例。燒猪吃否不須提。

兩心契。便許婚為婿。

雌飛直欲與雄齊。守貞翻嗤循古禮。

道德嫌拘泥。嬌娃縱莫制。

JSGJ II.1a

*In Cantonese wedding customs, the roasted pig
symbolizes the bride's virginity. After the marriage is
consummated, the groom's family sends a roasted pig
to the bride's family in recognition of her virginity.
Otherwise, the bride's chastity is in doubt and disputes
follow.

129 I married an emancipated woman,
    Who flexes her tigress might.
    What can I do about harmony in the bedroom?
    She has no fear of lectures from the pillow side.
    For her, they are so much wind.
    She talks back all the more.
    It's a repeat of the lioness roaring at the eastern
      riverbank.*
    O, how did that Gwaiseung ever have any fun?†

娶着自由女。拓張脂虎威。
蘭房不睦若何如。角枕教訓毫不懼。
當作吹。還重口嘴嘴(一)。
獅吼河東再復遇。李常那有樂歡娛。
（一）口嘴嘴：頂撞多説話

JSGJ II.35a

  *"Lioness' roar at the eastern riverbank" alludes to a wife's outrage at and domination over her husband, usually seen as negative in the man's viewpoint.
  †Gwaiseung (Chen Jichang) is a legendary henpecked husband who lived in fear under the ruthless dictates of his wife.

130　A Chinese woman follows Western ways,
　　Accepting none of her husband's remonstrations,
　　O, how can there be the conjugal harmony of fish
　　　　and water?*
　　She absolutely disdains the Three Classics and
　　　　the Six Rites.†
　　Flexing her status and her might,
　　Ignoring her notorious reputation,
　　She puts on strange and colorful clothes, acting
　　　　cute and charming;
　　She would trade her flesh to make a living.

華婦行西例。概不受夫制。

怎能魚水得和諧。絕念三書和六禮。

倚權勢。弗顧名聲壞。

服色異裝賽俏儷。甘將皮肉作生涯。

JSGJ II.23a

　　*"Fish and water" alludes to a perfect marital relationship.
　　†The "Three Classics" were the three major classics for Chinese women to cultivate a virtuous womanhood: *Nü jie* (Regulations for Women), *Nü lunyu* (Woman's Analects), and *Neixun* (Domestic Lectures); the "Six Rites" were the six proper steps to follow in a traditional marriage arrangement, from initial proposal to wedding ceremony.

131 These young women, with their rouge-darkened
      brows,
   At last, they're all freed from their confining boudoirs.
   No longer needing matchmakers to arrange their
      marriages;
   They go out together, hand-in-hand, seeking out
      handsome men.
   They are all lovely,
   Endowed with sensuous charms.
   From afar, I thought they were *peipa* girls;*
   Who would have guessed they are actually fine
      maidens!

這樣紅粉黛。深閨特別開。
終身大事不須媒。携手同行尋靚仔(一)。
令人愛。大有風情在。
遠觀疑是琵琶妹(二)。誰知香閨小粧台。

(二)(一)
琵靚
琶仔
妹：
：參
歌看
妓歌
，＃
指26
妓
女

JSGJ II.3a

*A *peipa* (*pipa*) girl is a song girl for hire, an enter-
tainer. Usually the term refers to a prostitute trained to
play the stringed musical instrument to entertain her
patrons.

132 The oppression of women has been around for a
        long, long time.
     So many women live in sorrow.
     Progress and civilization are gradually removing
        the restrictions.
     So, let's stretch out and free our minds; no more
        suffocation!
     Wisdom unfolds,
     Acquiring knowledge of East and West through
        education.
     Equality has been won, and must be maintained.
     How can we tolerate the confines of those dated
        moral conventions?

閨閣專制耐。多少美人哀。

進化文明遂撤裁。舒暢胸懷靡窒礙

智慧開。學堂通中外。

博得平權態度在。不堪閫範守從來。

JSGJ II.3a

133 We are all charming and refined;
We don't submit ourselves to oppression.
Sisters, let's have a good time together;
Who'll dare criticize us for wearing different
and colorful clothes?
What's there to fear?
Let's hang around here and there, everywhere.
We'll ignore the street gossip and slanderous
remarks;
We are all as pure as white jade, without a blemish
whatsoever.

我等嬌姿雅。專制不從他。

何妨姊妹共繁華。服色異裝誰敢話(一)。

怕乜(二)呀。縱橫到處要。

弗管街談謗毀也。儼如白璧本無瑕。

(一)話：批評斥責

(二)怕乜：怕什麼

JSGJ II.3a

134 In all earnestness, I speak to all my sisters:
Why be so easily discouraged?
From now on, superior talents will arise among
us women;
Men and women will have equal rights, and that
will not change!
Won't that be wonderful?
A life without oppression!
We can choose our own mate, be he a wise man
or a fool.
Even our parents can't interfere with us anymore!

敬告眾姊妹。何必心先灰。
從今巾幗起高才。男婦平權無更改。
得意哉。身處專制外。
夫婿智愚隨我採。縱然爹媽阻唔來(一)。

（一）阻唔來：阻止不了

JSGJ II.2a

135 Following the practice of the Western countries,
I am free to make my marriage choice.
I cheer that the obsolete rituals are abolished.
No longer can matchmakers manipulate our lives.
It's a brand new world.
I am married in a civilized way.
I have found a good husband on my own, as I have
      wished.
Our hearts and views are at one, our brows beam
      with joy.

取法泰西例。隨我結夫妻。

革除古禮實歡懷。免使媒婆來舞弊。

新世界。文明諧伉儷(一)。

在己如意迷佳婿。同心同德樂眉齊。

（一）
儷：作「儷」

JSGJ II.2b

136 Living in this Flowery Flag Nation,
  Marriage is by our own decision.
  The laws don't let even our parents break us
    apart—
  A pair of mandarin ducks or two entwined trees.*
  Remember this firmly:
  We have secretly vowed our matrimony.
  Someday, as we sing in harmony in our bedroom,
  We'll laugh that we were way ahead of our time.

他日唱隨繡閣裡。解嘲同話早知機。

記復記：秦晉秘定矣。

例非父母可拆離。比翼鴛鴦連理樹

身旅花旗地。婚姻自主持。

JSGJ II.32b

*"Mandarin ducks" and "entwined trees" allude to
conjugal happiness.

137 What a batch of lousy broads,
All without proper upbringing.
They hustle in the doorways, their gold teeth on
  parade;
Day and night, always going to the picture show.
They are fearless.
They laugh with lust and speak the barbarian tongue.
With men, they are experts at fooling around.
Alas, their dissipation is shameful to our China.

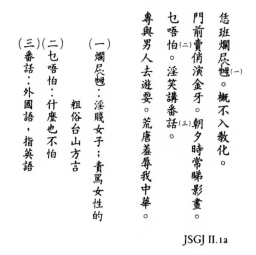

恁班爛尽姆。概不入教化。
門前賣俏演金牙。朝夕時常睇影畫。
乜唔怕。淫笑講番話。
專與男人去遊耍。荒唐羞辱我中華。

(三)番話∶外國語，指英語
(二)乜唔怕∶什麼也不怕
(一)爛尽姆∶淫賤女子；責罵女性的
　　　　　　粗俗台山方言

JSGJ II.1a

138   The beautiful lass, an American-born,
     A barbaric little princess.
     She follows the Western example and lives the
        American way;
     She doesn't accept her parents' strict discipline.
     Harboring high ideals,
     She chooses her own mate.
     Falling in love with one who shares her likes,
     She agrees to have sex with him before picking out
        the wedding day.

佳人生在美。便作小蠻姬。
倚爲西例效花旗。不受爹娘嚴管理。
立志氣。選婿從自己。
愛個相行情與義。約同交合訂婚期。

JSGJ II.1b

139 A gorgeous girl, of marriageable age, waiting for a
   proposal,
   Pretending to believe in Jesus' gospel.
   She falls head over heels for a pretty-faced young
   lad;
   They stroll together, hand-in-hand; their infatuation
   is mutual.
   Imitating the barbarian women,
   She plays house with him at her pleasure.
   Her parents might be furious, but what does she
   care;
   She wants a dandy, not her parents to interfere.

阿嬌年待字。假話信耶穌。

情牽靚仔好頭顱。携手同行相愛慕。

效蠻姑。隨意做夫婦。

縱有爹娘由佢怒。專制唔受摳登徒。

JSGJ II.2a

140 My heart belongs to a handsome young lad.
  We exchange messages in English letters.
  Sixteen is a peach blossom that's just about to bud;
  O, how I long to share his pillow!
  Lips meeting,
  Like the union of Cowherd and Weaving Maid.*
  The passion of clouds and rain is thick as glue.†
  We make another date to meet in the evening after
   an interlude.

靚仔奴心遂。番信⁽一⁾寄通語。
二八桃花初開蕊。但得與他同枕睡。
咀合咀。儼然牛女會。
雲雨情濃如膠水。約定黃昏再復回。

（一）番信：：英文書信

JSGJ II.32b

*In Chinese mythology, the Heavenly Queen
Mother separated the celestial couple, the Cowherd
and the Weaving Maid, because their infatuation inter-
fered with their jobs. They were given the opportunity
to have a reunion once a year at the Milky Way, on the
seventh day of the seventh lunar month.
 †"Clouds and rain," see song 42.

141 All dolled up, strolling along the street.
     She's so elegant and sweet!
     She dresses half Chinese, half American,
     She ties her loose temple hair with a bright silk
        ribbon.
     She shows her fashion expertise,
     Not her feminine disposition.
     Women nowadays are different from those in the past;
     They follow their own preferences now in choosing a
        husband.

扮靚遊街巷。娉婷的有當(一)
半成華派半西裝。鬢尾鬆鬆絹艷緔(二)
演在行。坤儀全不講。
繡閣世風今異往。任隨己意選檀郎。

(二)(一)
的扮
當靚
：：
適打
合扮
潮漂
流亮

JSGJ II.1a

142 Native-borns call each other brother and sister.
They live in the American way.
Holding hands, they say they're off to a picture
  show.
Actually, they're going to a hotel!
Enjoying their longings and desires,
So what if people gossip;
The two of them entwined in deep passion;
She may become pregnant, but that's nothing strange!

土產稱兄姊。俗例效花旗。^(一)

相同携手話睇戲。實係行去旅館住。

悦心痴^(二)。唔怕人論恥。

兩家攬埋爽入味。雖然大肚不爲奇。

（一）土產：土生
（二）攬埋：擁抱在一起

SEVEN

Nuptial Rhapsodies

According to Cantonese folklore, a man's highest achievement is *dang fo* (*deng ke*), meaning "advancement to the honor roll." Specifically, a man had two opportunities in life to *dang fo*. The first is the *daai dang fo* ("major advancement"), in which he successfully passed the highest level of the imperial examination and was proclaimed the best scholar in the imperial honor roll. This could be achieved only through intellectual pursuits. The other, *siu dang fo* ("minor advancement"), happened on the wedding night, when the groom would finally meet his bride to consummate their marriage. "Major advancement" was a man's top honor in the Confucian society, bringing great prestige and glory to the family name, but few could attain it. "Minor advancement" was more accessible. To the family, it was equally significant, because for a man to continue the family line was an important responsibility. Every man could achieve his "minor advancement" when he got married. The marriage was treated as the most important event of his life, and it would be duly recorded in the family registry.

Through the social institution of marriage, a man's masculinity was publicly acknowledged and his manhood recognized. Thus, Cantonese folklore places emphasis on man's sexuality, which represents not just his social responsibility to the family but also his transition from son to husband, from childhood to manhood. The wedding night is the testimony of this ascension to manhood.

These Chinatown rhymes on nuptial bliss are an interesting group of writings, given the reality that many of the Chinese immigrants were married but lived without their wives in the United States. In these compositions, the immigrants act out their sexual and marital fantasies through writing, in Western terms, using creative writing as a form of sublimation. By indulging in fantasies about his sexuality on the wedding night, the man is making a declaration of his manhood, despite being deprived of his normal sexual relationship with his wife during his American sojourn. Furthermore, the assumption of a feminine persona in some of the rhymes serves merely to affirm a man's erotic and sexual desires in a marital relationship. However, a few rhymes on this theme contain statements about the practice of polygamy that show a modern Western influence, and recognize marriage as an equal relationship between man and woman.

143   Seeing the moon is but an added vexation.
      A full moon brings back memories:
      The Moon Festival, a clamorous celebration;*
      The moon, round and clear, is at its best this evening.
      To the moon I pray:
      Where is the Old Man from the Moon?†
      I have yet to meet a woman of moon-faced charm.
      In a solitary window, the bright moonlight—my spirit
        sinks all the more.

望月添煩惱。月圓就想到。
期逢賞月聲嘈嘈。皎皎月輪斯宵好。
對月告。憑誰爲月老。
月貌佳人唔得倒(一)。孤窗明月倍神勞。

（一）唔得倒：不能獲得

JSGJ I.49b

*That is, the "Mid-autumn Festival," the fifteenth
day of the eighth lunar month, a festival of love and
reunions. Cf. song 92.

†"Old Man from the Moon" is a mythical deity, a
matchmaker.

144 Beside the Peony Pavilion,*
By chance I met a lady visitor.
Her charm and grace, all beyond pen's description;
Her dress, white as snowflakes.
So unique and special.
I am aroused thinking of her all the time.
Constantly yearning for her, with passionate
admiration,
O, I can't let go of the thought of her; I just can't
let it go!

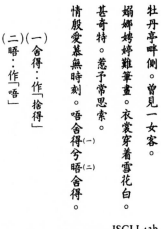

JSGJ I.43b

*A reference to the famous Ming dynasty drama
Peony Pavilion (*Mudan ting*) by Tang Xianzu (1550–
1616), about the meeting and secret rendezvous of a
scholar and a young woman.

145 I was hooked by that woman dressed in white.
My spirit held captive, as if intoxicated.
At home, sitting by the window, the more I think
of her, the more captivated I am.
O, I've fallen in love and can't share with her my
admiration.
I constantly think of her,
I can't sleep the whole night.
I only wish to meet her again in the garden,*
Where we will sing happily together in the
moonlight.

掛住白衣女。令我神如醉。
歸窗越想越痴愚(一)。為姐相思難解語。
記緊佢。一夜唔曾睡。
只望花園能復遇。共娘月下樂倡隨(二)。

(二)(一)
倡唔
：曾
作：
「沒
唱有
」

JSGJ I.43b

*In Tang Xianzu's *Peony Pavilion* (see song 144),
there is a scene entitled "A Sudden Dream in the Gar-
den" in which the young heroine, in her dream, meets
the young scholar and they have a pre-marital relation-
ship.

146 I am at the age of waiting for a marriage proposal.
Naturally I desire a fine man.
To start, I write a message on a red leaf,* and
enjoin the matchmaker:
My heart admires not just any young dandy, be he
smart and handsome.
Please, set your mind to the task.
Take your time, check him out to total satisfaction.
If he is talented, well versed in the classics and
histories,
I could care less about his appearance.

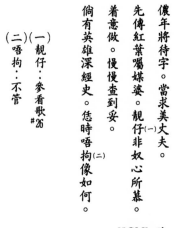

倘有英雄深經史。怎時唔拘像如何(二)。

着意做。慢慢查到妥。

先傳紅葉囑媒婆。靚仔(一)非奴心所慕。

儂年將待字。當求美丈夫。

（二）唔拘：不管
（一）靚仔：參看歌#26

JSGJ II.38b

*"Red leaf" is a symbol used in marriage proposal
rituals. It originated in a Tang dynasty tale in which a
palace maid wrote a message on a red (maple?) leaf
expressing her desire to be married. The leaf floated
down the palace canal and was picked up by a young
man, who later became her husband.

147 A handsome lad, though fair and fine,
Does not compare to a man of talent.
With good looks but no skills, life is nothing but
   toil.
But if he is fluent in Chinese speech and American
   ways,
And has high ambition,
He can make a living in commerce or government.
His works will win everyone's praises.
Why then judge a man by his hair and skin at such a
   moment?

靚仔(一)雖則好。莫如才子高。

有貌無能週世勞。若曉唐文和番道(二)。

志氣囂。直同官商撈(三)。

假手做來人贊(四)好。恁時何必論皮毛。

（一）靚仔：參看歌 #26

（二）番道：西方的風俗及做事方式

（三）撈：交易來往

（四）贊：作「讚」

JSGJ II.38a

148 Finally, we are wed.
Never before have I shared a word with my man.*
A stealthy glance at my groom, dazed and delighted;
O, how I wonder about tonight's happy moment.
I must be a complete fool—
Not following the emancipated women,
Not sharing a bed sooner with my handsome man,
To wait until today for this paired arrangement!

之子始于歸。未曾通一語。
偷看新郎痴似醉。不知今晚樂何如。
真係贅(一)。唔學自由女。
早與佳兒同衾睡。等到今日始成對。

（一）贅：笨

JSGJ I.42a

*In traditional China, newlyweds met each other
for the first time after completing the public wedding
ceremony. They were often total strangers before that
moment since their marriage was arranged by parents
through a matchmaker.

149 The young man, in joyous song of the peach,*
The bride's charm radiates under the glow of
    wedding candles.
Happy their first meeting in the bedroom.
Tenderly they talk, sharing their hearts.
The beautiful woman's wish:
Smilingly, softly, she speaks—
At midnight, our union is consummated with utmost
    delight;
Inside the hibiscus tent, my regret is to have waited
    so long to marry.†

桃夭賦之子。花燭艷嬌姿。
蘭房初會樂怡怡。細把素心談彼此。
美人意。含笑輕啓齒。
半夜合歡歡不已。芙蓉帳裡恨歸遲。

JSGJ I.26b

   * "Peach" alludes to courtship and nuptial bliss. This
usage originates from the Confucian classic *Shi jing*, the
first anthology of Chinese poetry.
   † "Hibiscus tent" implies the act of love and sexual
intimacy, as seen in the Tang narrative poem "Chang
hen ge" ("Everlasting Sorrow") by Bo Juyi (772–846),
which depicts the romance of Emperor Ming of Tang
(Xuanzong) and his consort Yang Guifei. See song 60.

150 Tenderly I share words with Husband,
Pleasantly enjoying the various delights.
The hibiscus tent is filled with happy moments;*
O, why didn't the nuptial bliss take place sooner?
I am as intoxicated as an apple blossom.
In our castle, we sleep entwined.
In union at night, deep in passion, lips meeting
lips,
O, this young woman regrets the belated match.

共郎細解語。含笑別樣趣。
芙蓉帳裡樂歡娛。着乜(一)桃夭唔早遇。
海棠醉。紫薇交頸睡。
夜合情濃咀合咀。美人還悔慢成對。

（一）着乜：爲何

JSGJ I.42a

*"Hibiscus tent," see song 149.

151 A lovely woman, sheltered in a gilded mansion.
     A nuptial union, celebrated under the bright lights
       of wedding candles.
     Furtively, his hands fondle her breasts;
     Modestly, she steals a glance at her groom.
     Their eyes come together.
     Fondly attracted, they loosen their clothes.
     Together they sleep, sharing pillow and bed—
     O, this is what I want to have; this is truly what I
       I want to have!

阿嬌藏金屋。洞房閙花燭。

安排手弄鷄頭肉。淑女偷看郎格局(一)。

兩關目。機投解衣服。

雙雙共枕同床宿。心所欲兮心所欲。

（一）
格局．儀態外貌

JSGJ I.26a

152   A beautiful woman, sheltered in a gilded mansion.
      A nuptial union, celebrated under the bright lights
        of wedding candles.
      Together we'd sleep, sharing pillow and bed.
      To my heart's content, I'd caress her tender breasts.
      O, moments such as this—
      I just don't know this joy that I can get.
      Instead I came to live alone in the West
      And betrayed sixteen years of my youthful best.

阿嬌藏金屋。洞房鬧花燭。

雙雙共枕同床宿。任爾手弄鷄頭肉。

當此局。都唔噲納福。

情願西來單寮獨。負了青春一十六。

JSGJ II.25b

153 Of all the joys in life,
The happiest is the nuptial hymn.
A young couple, man and wife, consummate their
conjugal tie.
A pair of lovebirds, sleeping together, necks
entwined.
Eyes meet—
Neither is accustomed to the dew of clouds and
rain.*
She is willing, yet shy; his spirit soars and dances.
A handsome man with a charming woman, O, what
would that joy be like?

人生歡喜事。最好桃天賦。
青年夫婦結絲羅(一)。一對鴛鴦交頸臥。
眼顧顧。未慣雲雨露。
欲就還推神飛舞。嬌娘才子樂如何。

（一）
羅：作「羅」

JSGJ I.25b

*"Clouds and rain," see song 42.

154 Such sensations are second to none:
Husband and wife indulging in each other's passion.
Celebrating the marvelous moment in the nuptial
chamber, under bright wedding candles,
Shyly she releases the gilded tent-hooks, sharing
the brocade quilt.
They act out a new play,
Truly fascinated.
The fifth watch strikes at early dawn, hurrying them
to rise.*
O, how can the entwined lovebirds ever separate?

五鼓相催思早起。鴛鴦交頸也難離。

演新戲。果然眞趣味。

洞房花燭鬧佳期。羞解金扣同錦被。

風流世莫比。夫妻兩美癡。

JSGJ I.25b

*A night in China was divided into five watches.
First watch: 7–9 P.M.; second watch: 9–11 P.M.; third
watch: 11 P.M. to 1 A.M.; fourth watch: 1–3 A.M.; fifth
watch: 3–5 A.M.

155 A nuptial union is a song of joy.
For the first time I met my blossom of the
wedding chamber.
A consummation at night, more exquisite than the most
gorgeous sight.
Her smiling profile, so refined.
O, sweet sixteen.
Inside the tent, the hibiscus is in full bloom.*
She sleeps, an apple blossom tired by spring passion.
At fifth watch she puts on her rouge and magnolia
cream.†

桃夭歌樂也。初賞洞房花。

雙雙夜合賽容華。半面含笑真大雅。

喜破瓜。帳裡芙蓉耍。

春睡海棠情欲罷。玉蘭脂粉五更搽。

JSGJ I.26b

*"Hibiscus tent," see song 149.
†"Fifth watch," see song 154.

156　Clouds and rain meet in the scented bedroom;*
Immense pleasure, the evening union.
The nuptial bliss, as chanted in the *Songs*, is the
　utmost joy;†
A good man and a virtuous wife—perfect harmony.
It's sheer intoxication;
Lovebirds begin to open their hearts.
The apple blossom sleeps well on a warm spring
　day.
Happy is the song of conjugal harmony within
　the hibiscus tent.‡

日暖海棠春足睡。芙蓉帳裡樂唱隨。
素心醉。鴛鴦初解語。
桃夭詩詠極歡娛。君子好逑諧淑女。
蘭房雲雨遇。夜合多情趣。

JSGJ I.25b

*"Clouds and rain," see song 42.
†"That is, the Confucian classic *Shi jing*; its first
section consists of folk songs of courtship and marriage.
‡"Hibiscus tent," see song 149.

157 Under painted wedding candles, the bride and
      groom unite.
   Of all delights, this is the best.
   Like rain clouds after a prolonged drought;
   Young and strong the groom, lovely and tender
      the bride.
   Within the nuptial chamber,
   Better than a thousand in gold is their wedding bliss.
   With untiring passion, the phoenix turns, the dragon
      whirls.*
   A word to the neighbor's rooster: don't crow too
      early in the morning!

花燭諧伉儷。襟懷最暢快。
恰如久旱見雲霓。男也丁年女少艾。
洞房際。風流千金抵(一)。
倒鳳顛鸞情弗懈。囑語鄰鷄勿早啼。

（一）
抵：值

JSGJ I.26a

*Dragon and phoenix represent groom and bride in
Cantonese wedding phrases.

158 Smiling, we sing to our nuptial union.
It begins with a poem written on a red leaf.*
The bliss of love, like fish in water, reaches up to
the brows;†
Inside the hibiscus tent, unrestrained is our passion.‡
A song of the peach.§
I am in harmony with two delights in the fragrant
bedroom:
Tonight, I've finally tasted the scent of rouge and
blossoms;
Next year, we will give birth to a son!

JSGJ I.26b

* "Red leaf," see song 146.
† "Fish and water," see song 130.
‡ "Hibiscus tent," see song 149.
§ "Song of the peach," see song 149.

159 Speaking of the fun of having wives:
You should have at least three or four—
The slender Feiyin on the left, the plump Yukwaan
　on the right,*
O, that would be heavenly, even better than
　immortal life.
Then, most provoking—
Suddenly a jealous wind starts to blow:
Number One refuses to take you in; and Number Two
　ignores you.
It's a hell of a long night in solitary.

講到老婆味。至少要三四。

左邊燕瘦右環肥。個的風流仙莫比(一)。

最激氣。酸風立地起。

大不收留二不理。那時長夜嘆凄其。

（一）
個的‧那般

JSGJ I.44a

* Allusions to Chinese beauties: Feiyin (Zhao Fei-yan) was a classic slender beauty; Yukwaan (Yang Yuhuan, or consort Yang Guifei) was her plump counterpart.

160 I've examined the marriage laws:
     The Western practice is the most civil.
     One man with one woman: happiness and harmony.
     Why in the world do Chinese men take in concubines
     And redeem their favorite prostitutes?
     Lust and greed are an insatiable lot.
     When concubines all fight to butter up the First Wife,
     They'll throw out the husband to sleep with only his
        pillow until the rooster crows.

嘗攷婚姻例。最合是泰西。

一男一女樂和諧。何事華人娶二奶(一)。

贖老契(二)。貪淫無了賴。

大小不停爭寵大。拋郎孤枕過鷄啼。

(一)二奶：妾

(二)老契：姘頭妓女

JSGJ I.44b

161　One man paired with one woman,
　　Love, not jealousy, will prevail.
　　For peace and quiet at home, this is the only way.
　　If you insist like a tyrant on taking a concubine,
　　And indulging in pretty young women,
　　How can you avoid your wife's lioness roar?*
　　You'll have to put up with her and suffer the pain.
　　Had you known what would happen today, how you
　　　　would have regretted your behavior.

斯時忍氣甘受苦。早知今日悔當初。

小艾慕。難免河東獅。

家室和平要如此。若恃強權娶妾婦。

一公配一婆。恩愛無嫉妒。

JSGJ I.44b

*"Lioness roar," see song 129.

EIGHT

Ballads of
the Libertines

Just as there has been a perennial controversy over the
artistic expression of nudity and pornography in West-
ern culture, in China, romancing a woman and woman-
izing for sheer sex have attracted similar attention. In
traditional Chinese literature, courtship and romance are
for the most part praised. Sex between lovers, even if
premarital, was championed as far back as the folk songs
of the *Shi jing* collection and the later *Yuefu* anthology.
Womanizing and the lust for sex, however, have been
regarded as excessive behavior and wicked indulgence.
Chinese legends and stories repeatedly tell of the destruc-
tion of families and kingdoms, as well as the destruction
of a man's future, because of the obsession for women
and sex.

In Cantonese folklore, womanizing is considered to
be one of the major vices, leading a man from a happy
and contented life to one of tragedy. In the Pearl River
delta region, womanizing was considered much like
opium smoking; it was a vice of the affluent class, since

less fortunate men could not afford the luxury of recklessly spending money on either women or opium. To occasionally socialize with loose women of the gay quarters was common and acceptable; but frequent patronization of these places was considered sinful. Men, both married and unmarried, were sternly and frequently warned of the harm associated with such illicit sex— the ruin of one's reputation and wealth and the diseases that could eventually cost a libertine his manhood and his ability to sire children. Thus, licentiousness was considered most unfilial, a betrayal of a man's duty and obligation to his family.

Many vernacular writings tell of adventures with women, with the final message that succumbing to lust would mean the downfall of everything else. Of course, like other writings that purport to have redeeming social value, these popular books were often actually quite pornographic, the pornography camouflaged by a didactic ending, a moral to serve as a "warning" to the audience. Such a treatment apparently satisfied Confucian didacticism, and made such works at least on the surface acceptable on the grounds of "moral education."

This type of vernacular literature was popular as well in early Chinatown. In book advertisements of the day, titles of such publications are listed side by side with those of dictionaries to learn English, sex manuals, and the Confucian classics. Alongside them, one might also notice the ads of physicians and pharmacists announcing cures and remedies for venereal diseases.

The tolerance of Chinatown residents toward pornographic writings extended to the early immigrants' own creative writings, for erotic and pornographic rhymes were published alongside the more serious rhymes. However, this phenomenon did not indicate that the population was full of sex fiends, nor that the men were wanton in their behavior. In reality, the acute absence of normal female companionship encouraged these "vices" to be regarded as something normal in the community. In this woman-less environment, expressions of immense sexual fantasy and deep interest in the opposite sex were natural. They also served to show how these desperate men attempted to compensate for living in an American community barren of normal sexual expression, and thus dramatize a social problem in Chinatown. What had been once perceived as a major vice in their own Cantonese upbringing became a necessity in their American existence, providing the immigrants with a temporary form of solace and an instant reminder of their manhood when life without female companionship appeared to be no life at all.

To the modern reader, these rhymes also provide a much-needed antidote to the stereotype of the early Chinese immigrants as a group of emasculated, morbid men lacking in expressions of sexual or any kind of human interest. On the contrary, these writings reveal a physically vibrant and often humorous group of people.

162 Life is a dream, an illusion:
　　A twenty-year span of fun and games.
　　Hugging the one in red, leaning on the one in green,
　　　O, what joy and gaiety!
　　Treasure the youthful years: once gone, they never
　　　return.
　　Before that time comes—
　　What man won't hanker after pretty faces
　　Like a butterfly lingering around lustrous flowers?
　　A death from passion is really nothing.

蝴蝶尚愛花燦爛。縱爲情死也當閒。
年未晚。誰不戀嬌顏。
偎紅倚翠幾風繁。可惜青春去不返。
人生和夢幻。快活廿年間。

JSGJ II.26b

163　At eighteen or twenty-two,
　　　Young man, don't forget:
　　　It's best to enjoy life when the time is right.
　　　Should you wait till old age comes, there won't be
　　　　　any more fun.
　　　Just think about this, each of you—
　　　All the singing and dancing in places of merriment.
　　　If you pretend to be upright and won't lay your finger
　　　　　on this,
　　　You're wasting a splendid moment and you are but a
　　　　　fool.

十八與廿二。後生勿忘記(一)。
及時行樂最便宜。待到老來冇趣味(二)。
各自思。歌舞繁華地。
若詐至誠唔染指。虛度韶光亦太癡。

（一）後生：年青人
（二）冇：參看歌
　　　#111

JSGJ II.25a

164 We're guests stranded in North America;
Must we also give up the fun in life?
Girls of the Flowery Flag Nation, all superbly
beautiful and charming;
By all means, have a taste of the white scent while
there's time.
If both sides are willing,
Why not share a dream in bed?
If you betray your youthful vigor and such
wonderful delight,
Just remember, you may return to the old country as a
wealthy man, but you won't have this chance again!

作客羈北美。行樂勿拋棄。

花旗⁽一⁾女子極標緻。及早當嘗白種味。

肯投機。與他同夢寐。

若負青春佳景地。有錢歸國再難期。

(一)
花旗：參看歌
#3

JSGJ II.26a

165 I've madly fallen for that woman.
No magic pills can cast away the love spell.
Her blossom-like appearance, charmingly made-up,
    a beauty unsurpassed—
O, how can I share her pillow?
For her,
My heart aches with deep anxiety.
Such a beautiful woman, but there's no way I can get
    her to be mine.
I only wish my soul would seek out her scented
    curtain in dreams.

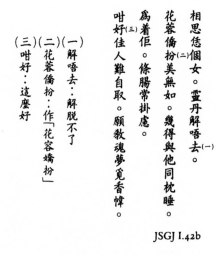

相思恁個女。靈丹解唔去⁽一⁾。
花容僑扮⁽二⁾美無如。幾得與他同枕睡。
為着佢。條腸常掛慮。
咁好佳人難自取。願教魂夢覓香幃⁽三⁾。

（一）解唔去：解脫不了
（二）花容僑扮：作「花容嬌扮」
（三）咁好：這麼好

JSGJ I.42b

166 Sweet sixteen, that's the right moment.
Happy times should not be lightly abandoned.
Youthful days, once they have slipped away, cannot be
detained.
Dear lady, do you realize this opportunity is golden?
A union of clouds and rain— *
Most wonderful at the young and tender age.
If you don't catch the fun while it's here,
It won't taste as sweet in later years.

破瓜該時候。樂事莫輕拋。
青春一往總難留。這段機緣卿悟否。
雲雨交。妙齡最精巧。
如弗早尋快活鬧。老來滋味少甜頭。

（一）
段：多作「段」

(一)

JSGJ II.26a

* "Clouds and rain," see song 42.

167 A demeanor truly charming and divine:
Her willow waist is slender and graceful;
Her steps, beneath her fitted silk skirt, are
leisurely;
Her hair, spread over her shoulders; her appearance,
a peerless splendor.
Overwhelmed by her charm,
I have fallen in love and I am haunted.
Her elegance is rare in the mortal world.
O, how can I spend the night with her, sharing
quilt and pillow!

姿事真窈窕。娟娜小蠻腰。
羅裙齊整步逍遙。頭髮拖肩容絕妙。
感阿嬌。相思魂夢繞。
大雅不凡塵世少。怎能衾枕伴同宵。

JSGJ I.35a

168 Who can surpass her charm and grace?
　　Her spirit is captivating, not just some coquettish
　　　play.
　　At the sight of her, what man's brows won't be
　　　raised?
　　Dandies follow her from behind; they drool and
　　　anticipate.
　　She is a rare beauty in any age!
　　There's just no comparison.
　　She wears a long tunic, covering her thighs;
　　O, she dresses so well, better than anyone else
　　　in the Flowery Flag Nation.

縹緻誰可比。傳神非喜戲。
執兔見佢不揚眉。白算(一)跟隨呑呫喇(二)。
古來稀。邊個有咁美。
衫亦放長凹過髀。渾身打扮賽花旗。

（一）白算：登徒子
（二）呑呫喇：垂涎不已
（三）邊個：參看歌#62

JSGJ I.36b

169 A man's ambition is to conquer the world.
He cannot let rouge and women bewitch him.
Admiration for the young and beautiful is natural;
    so what can he do?
Escape from their tender demands and intimate bonds
    is just impossible.
Stranded in the realm of lust,
You've stayed in the paradise of comfort far too
    long;
You may have the might to move mountains,
But you must bow to the fragrant curtain that
    blocks your way.

丈夫氣蓋世。紅粉豈能迷。
無奈人情慕少艾。軟索緊纏終莫擺。
困色界。溫柔鄉久滯。
任爾拔山霸力大。香幃攔住也頭低。

JSGJ I.5a

170 I have seen action in war a hundred million times;
    I can move swiftly around battlefronts with habitual
      ease.
    To destroy enemy troops and behead their general is
      a simple, effortless task;
    I can go on a rampage, without fear whatsoever.
    But, once trapped among flowers—
    I am indolent despite my power.
    Unable to free myself from the layered curtains
      in the kingdom of fragance,
    My unusual prowess all becomes ordinary and
      unspectacular.

交鋒千百萬。陣門走動慣。
斬將破敵有何難。到處橫行無忌憚。
陷花間。本事就懶慢。
香國重幃惡解散。全身八寶亦當閒。

(一)
惡：難；參看歌 #12

JSGJ I.5b

171 Once inside the labyrinthian cave,
Even a heroic man would lose his mighty demeanor.
So many brave men are held captive amidst flowers:
Souls and spirits bewitched, unable even to turn.
In a palace of beautiful women,
Can anyone boast of his wisdom and might?
Indulging in the love of flowers, with no caution
or care,
He could not escape this prison cage even if he had the
ability to fly.

一入迷魂洞。豪傑失威風。
好漢多少困花叢。被他喪神譽(一)轉動。
粉黛宮。誰能稱智勇。
花貪風流唔慎重。飛天本事被牢籠。

（一）譽：難，參看歌#10

JSGJ I.5a

172 The gorgeous woman is just too much;
Her tender passion is a tiger-cage prison.
With an army I challenge her, showing her the
    weapons.
To my surprise, I am flattened by her soft,
    whirling whips.
Soar no more;
A defeated general stranded on a narrow path.
Water flows from the ravine, flooding the grass.
O, how can a powerless man make his escape?

艷色母太好。柔情等虎牢。

軍挑娘子逞干戈。竟被軟鞭來壓例(一)。

飛不高。敗將困夾道。

溝水潺潺深沒草。問君無力怎能逃。

（一）例：作「倒」

JSGJ. I.5b

173 Wandering into an array of flowers and wine,*
Spending thousands for the love of flowers,
Flower debts are endless;
It's better to live a straight life, away from flowers:
No more a heart of the flower;†
No more indulgence in flowers;
In flying steps, I leap out of the flower bushes;
Bidding flowers farewell, I make up my mind to
return to farming.

飛步跳出花叢圍。辭花立志歸耕田。

花心變。再不尊花戀。

花債無底烏能填。莫若棄花從正便。

蕩入花酒陣。因花花萬千。

JSGJ I.8b

*An array, literally, a military formation in preparation for battle, here refers to the danger of involving oneself with women.
†"A heart of the flower" is a Cantonese idiom for a fickle and unfaithful lover, usually a man.

174 I almost ended up begging with a bowl.
What's this talk about having a good time with
women?
My savings are exhausted; what choice is there for me?
How can I even speak of a rendezvous with fragrance?
I'd rather remain as this inept self,
Bearing hunger and enduring thirst.
I am cut off from the wild world of flowers and wine,
Away from ten thousand kinds of crazes and passions.

幾乎要托鉢(一)。講乜野(二)快活。
床頭金盡難裁奪。那有尋芳這一說。
甘守拙。捱飢兼抵渴。
迫從酒地花天闊。萬種癡情都忍割。

（一）托鉢：行乞
（二）乜野：什麼

JSGJ II.25b

175 Well fed, warmly clothed; next comes desire and
    passion.
Get a woman and shelter her in a gilded mansion.
But I am broke and constantly toiling;
How can I think of loving fragrance and indulging
    myself in jade?
Trapped in this impoverished valley—
Bowels twist in sorrow, brows twitch in pain.
To live without pleasure is to be a piece of wood or a
    clod of dirt.
Yet, with not even a grain to eat at home, what can
    a man do?

飽煖思淫慾。買姬藏金屋。

我乏錢財勞碌碌。奚理憐香兼惜玉。

困窮谷。腸愁額又蹙。

快樂拋離如土木。家裡奈因無粒粟。

JSGJ II.25a

NINE

Songs of the Young at Heart

In old China, a male-dominated, gerontocratic society, a man of advanced age commanded respect, authority, and special privileges. It was acceptable for a man of wealth and nobility to have more than one wife and common for him to acquire one or more concubines to "entertain" him during his retirement. Moreover, instead of scandalizing his neighbors, he would be known as "an old man but young at heart" (*ren lao fengliu*). Of course such a society was extremely unfair to women, as the latter were not accorded similar privileges. In such a gerontocracy, young women became the means by which "old fools" recaptured their lost youth and reclaimed the youthful spirit and vitality that was contradicted by their chronological age. Not having a young one beside him would be an admission that an old man's days were numbered. With her by his side, he might be an old fool, but he was young at heart. He still had energy and vitality of life; chronological age did not matter.

The Chinese Exclusion Act of 1882 left many Chinese workers stranded in the United States. They were afraid that if they ever made a short visit to China, new American immigration regulations would not allow them to return. Thousands upon thousands of those who had come as laborers during the earlier period were sent back to China, either voluntarily or involuntarily, under the exclusion provisions. For them, leaving the United States meant losing their means of economic survival. Those who could not afford to go home permanently dared not leave at all. Those who had married before coming to the United States faced prolonged separations until they earned enough to finance a journey home. But those who had not married faced lifelong bachelorhood. This situation persisted until after the 1906 earthquake and fire, when some immigrants were able to claim the status of native-borns, hence obtaining the right to return to the United States. In the late 1890s, there was a large population of older Chinese men in Chinatown. Unlike their countrymen who settled in the deep South and married outside of their race, these Chinatown men had few social opportunities. They were the true bachelors of this bachelor society. With their deaths, their generation simply died off.

Some of them finally made sufficient financial gain. Many of these older men decided to go back to China for good, realizing that their only alternative would be to die a lonely death in the United States. The return of the older *Gamsaan haak* (*Jinshan ke*) or "sojourners from Gold Mountain" led to a common nuptial phenomenon in the Pearl River delta starting in the 1880s. It was commonly known as *ga lou long* (*jia lao lang*), meaning "to wed an older groom"—marriage between an older returnee and a young woman. Of course, behind this marriage relationship lay an economic incentive, a hefty dowry from the groom to the bride's parents. The young woman was thus merchandise in exchange. It was not uncommon for a returnee groom to be scores of years older than his bride. This was truly a cynical version of a young woman marrying for "maturity" and "security." For the man, such a marriage meant winning a trophy. His long years of hard work abroad had finally been rewarded by marriage to a young woman. His youthful manhood, much of which was lost in his prolonged stay in America, was reclaimed.

Not much is known about the life of those early bachelors who remained in Chinatown. These vernacular rhymes about the older men's womanizing craze, written in the early 1910s, are perhaps the only extant pieces of creative writing by members of that generation about themselves. They vividly bring to life the fantasies of these older men, as they, recognizing that they have lost their youth, desperately try to make up for lost time via the companionship of their young brides.

176 It's a darn shame just talking about it.
I'm already eighty this year.
For my whole life, I have despised going around to
    brothels;
Never once did I make myself a foolish john
    among whores.
I must be under a spell;
Why have I become so restless lately?
At this old age, I don't seem to know what to do
    with my life;
And now, I am totally taken by the sight of
    flowers.

講來都失禮。今年八十齊。
平生最憎打水圍(一)。亦無做過波蘿鷄。
真撞鬼(二)。因何咁嘈閉(三)。
臨老就唔得過世(四)。至到今日被花迷。

（一）圍：作「圍」；打水圍：亦作「打茶圍」，
　　　　在妓院作樂
（二）撞鬼：見鬼
（三）嘈閉：吵鬧不安
（四）唔得：不能

JSGJ I.17a

177   I've lived more than half of a century.
Only now do I start chasing after skirts.
Dressed like a handsome lad, I take a stroll along the
    willow lanes.*
When I spot a lovely face, thoughts whirl in my mind,
Heart throbs.
I must come up with a clever scheme:
If I could only redeem the fair one all for myself;
This old fool would be willing to empty his purse of
    silver and gold.

年已大半百。始學偷香客。
扮成靓仔遊柳陌。瞥見嬌顏多思索。
心勒勒。想條妙計策。
若使佳人能贖得。老夫願傾囊黃白。

（一）
柳陌：指柳巷；花街柳巷：
妓院

JSGJ I.16b

* "Willow lanes"—brothels.

178 The pair of mandarin ducks is wrongly matched.*
Their age difference is way too great:
An eighty-year-old grandpa, with his eighteen-
year-old wife—
Why, why such a nice young lass married to such an
old fellow?
And that long beard of his!
O, you should be ashamed of yourself in front
of the young woman.
I ask you, in the nupital suite, under the bright
wedding candles,
What can become of a rouge-faced woman with a
white-haired man?

鴛鴦配錯譜。年紀差得多。

八十公公十八婆。咁好佳人嫁伯父⁽一⁾。

兩筆鬚。應慚對少婦。

試問洞房花燭事。紅顏白髮果如何。

（一）伯父：年老男人

JSGJ I.18a

* "Mandarin ducks," see song 49.

179 A rouge-faced young woman weds a white-haired
        old man,
     What can she do with such a marriage arrangement?
     Husband, already many years past sixty;
     Wife, barely sixteen, a fine maiden.
     Alas, cut out the long-winded fuss!
     You, have you had enough fun with women?
     In this arranged marriage, she could not put in a word
        of her own;
     It's a fair bet that compatibility and love were never
        once of concern.

紅顏配白叟。嫁着有能較(一)。

檀郎甲子已回頭。二八佳人成匹偶。

少長撈(一)。風流知足否。

婚姻憑媒難開口。料無意合與情投。

（一）冇能較：參看歌#2

（二）撈：嘥唆

JSGJ I.19b

180 My head is going completely bald;
I am marrying the charming young one.
This marriage is supposedly my prayers come
  true;
Who would expect that she is disgruntled over
  my age so advanced?
When we retire to bed,
She always turns her buttocks toward me,
As if she is angry, all the time like this;
O, how can I get her to just compromise and have
  some fun?

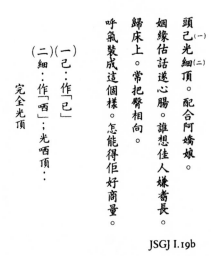

頭己光細頂。配合阿嬌娘。
姻緣佔話遂心腸。誰想佳人嫌壽長。
歸床上。常把臀相向。
呼氣裝成這個樣。怎能得佢好商量。

(一)
(二)(一)
細：作「哂」；光哂頂：
己：作「巳」
完全光頂

(一)己光細頂
(二)

JSGJ I.19b

181 I look like a pickled plum
When I marry a woman of willowy charm.
I was late in meeting this fine partner to tie the
lover's knot;
In the nuptial chamber, under bright wedding
candles, she's the very answer to my prayers.
I'm bent as an old pine tree.
In excitement, I turn to her happily.
I'm most afraid that she'll resent my old age.
Inside the hibiscus tent, no negotiation is deemed
necessary.*

最怕蘭閨嫌尊長。芙蓉帳裡少商量。
蒼松樣。喜得含笑向。
晚逢佳耦結鴛鴦。洞房花燭真合想。
貌似霜梅像。始配柳嬌娘。

JSGJ I.18b

*"Hibiscus tent," see song 149.

182   A shrunken old man am I,
Lucky enough to marry a young and lovely woman.
Don't ever laugh that a man in his late years has no
    talent;
The nuptial union under brilliant candlelight is
    celebrated in cheer.
Marvelous, isn't it?
A wonderful union consummated tonight.
My hair is white, but my vitality, like spring;
My lips on her rouged face, I love her all the more.

雖屬亞公仔(一)。猶幸阿嬌配。

漫笑年暮冇人才(二)。花燭洞房高喝彩。

得意哉。良緣今晚會。

白頭春事依然在。嘴交紅粉倍恩愛。

（一）公仔：年老男人

（二）冇人材：沒有才能

JSGJ I.18b

183 At first I thought it might not be fun:
An old man paired with a young woman.
It's not exactly a perfect match in the bedroom,
Yet it turns out like fish and water, our brows
    beaming in joy!*
As long as we like each other,
Why bother with our age?
Marriage is predestined in a former life;
I tease my young love, born just a bit late.

祇估冇趣味。伯爹配小姬。

誰知魚水樂齊眉。雖則房中非兩美。

合意氣。何必計年紀。

姻緣有譜前生註。戲笑細君出世遲。

JSGJ I.18a

* "Fish and water," see song 130.

184 Indeed my age is advanced—
A withered willow tree, but growing new wands.
Like a young lad, wearing a pair of fancy shoes,
I enter the nuptial suite and consummate the
    wedding rites.
I am satisfied,
Having a young and beautiful wife.
I pray that Heaven will look upon me with special
    favor:
Let me live a hundred years before we part!

雖則年紀邁。枯楊幸生梯。

猶如童子着花鞋。走入洞房成婚禮。

安樂細〔一〕。得個美少艾。

但願皇天另眼睇。賜吾百歲亦和諧。

（一）細：作「哂」；安樂哂：很滿足
安心了

JSGJ I.19a

185 I'm sixty, this autumn.
White hair on my temples, but I am not worried.
I dress in red and green, all fine silk;
When I walk, my body moves like a bending willow.
I indulge in wine,
And seek out a playmate in Laamkung.*
Tipsy, I turn to Seung Ngo and examine her fine
    details.†
The clouds and rain atop Wu Mountain are the
    wonders of making love.‡

重逢甲子秋。鬢白不知憂。
穿紅着綠又穿綢。舉步身搖如擺柳。
性嗜酒。臨邛尋愛友。
醉向嫦娥細研究。巫山雲雨樂優游。

JSGJ I.16b

  *In a Han dynasty anecdote, and later in popular
tales, the talented scholar Sima Xiangru (ca. 179–
117 B.C.) and Zhuo Wenjun, the widowed daughter of
the rich and powerful noble Zhuo Wangsun, eloped to
Laamkung (Linqiong) to live together without her
father's blessing. However, the reference here to Lin-
qiong is to a place of loose women, namely prostitutes.
  †"Seung Ngo," see song 56.
  ‡"Clouds and rain" and "Wu Mountain," see
song 42.

186 An old man am I: crane-white hair, weather-beaten,
Face wrinkled like a rooster's layered skin.
I am indeed an old crow, but with a desire to linger
around nests of magpies
And to enjoy my last years paired like mandarin ducks
in the wild.*
Like a homeless pigeon
I look for a pleasure mate by moonlight.
The gaily dressed orioles and swallows cover up
their mouths to hide their giggles;
Dear ladies, don't you laugh at my white hair!

鶴髮蒼顏叟。面似雞皮縐。
老鴉偏貪戀鵲巢。露宿鴛鴦著景樂。
形類鳩。月明尋歡偶。
紅粉燕鶯齊掩口。粧台莫笑我白頭。

JSGJ I.16b

* "Mandarin ducks," see song 49.

187 Already senile, still hanging around the north alley,*
Embracing young women and paying for their smiles,
Instantly forgetting his wrinkled skin and crane-white
hair,
Once bewitched by the charm of foxy women.
Like a starving hawk,
Enjoying the taste of the wild—
Hugging the beautiful one, not ashamed of his
hunched back.
What a lovely sight is an old man, walking cane in
hand, leaning on a young and lovely woman.

龍鐘遊北里。買笑擁雛姬。
頓忘鶴髮與鶉皮。一旦遭逢狐戲媚。
恍鷹飢。野鶩嘗滋味。
駝背否慚偎彼美。最憐鳩杖倚蛾眉。

JSGJ I.16a

* "North alley" refers to a red-light district.

188 So, just follow your impulse:
Enjoy the company of a beautiful woman.
With enough money, you can shelter the beauty
in a gilded mansion;
With too much indulgence your back will become
hunched and waist bent.
Obsessed with lust,
Spending nights in the whorehouses much too
often;
Don't you ever worry about your age, a lit candle
in a gusty wind?
You don't know your limits, you just don't!

而從心所欲。尚戀美人局。

多則阿嬌藏金屋。弄得駝背又腰曲。

好色慾。往往娼寮宿。

唔顧年幾當風燭。不知足兮不知足。

（一）娼寮：妓院

（二）幾：作「紀」

JSGJ I.16a

189 I never tire of the lust for women;
   At seventy, what do I care about destiny.
   Loose with passion, wild with desire, just like
      my younger days,
   Brothels and whorehouses are places of my
      mad indulgence.
   Am I a crazy old fool?
   But I do care if people see me there.
   So, I'd rather hide myself amidst beautiful
      flowers, look around to my heart's content,
   And ask every lovely creature to spend the night
      as my companion.

嗜淫心未倦。七十不知天。
縱情肆慾比英年。妓館娼寮志貪戀。
發老癲。恐怕人見面。
潛入花叢飽眼癮。偏求淑女伴同眠。

JSGJ I.17b

190 With this long beard already reaching to my belly,
You wouldn't think I'd be affected by lust or
desire.
But I'm still chasing after fragrant skirts;
Leaning on my cane, bent and bowed, I make love
with women.
A solace to my dire wishes—
The sisters celebrate my longevity with a banquet.
A white-haired man with blushing young women, all
drink to the Golden Valley,*
O, that's a heavenly life, don't you agree?

鬚已長過腹。只話忘色慾。

乃向羣芳肆微逐。策杖偷香躬又鞠。

慰衷曲。姊妹壽延祝(一)。

白髮紅顏醉金谷。汝話享福唔享福。

(一)延：作「筵」
(二)話：參看歌 #14

JSGJ I.17a

* "Golden Valley" refers to the Golden Valley Villa
built by the wealthy Shi Chong (A.D. 249–300) of the
Jin dynasty, where Shi entertained his beloved Lüzhu.

191   Searching for the Peach Blossom Cave,*
      This old man asks for directions.
      He comes to the kingdom of fragrance and visits
         the charming faces;
      He entertains himself with clouds and rain among
         the flowers.†
      Amidst the beautiful bushes,
      He teases at will, like a butterfly.
      The tender petals, soft and light, emit a heavy
         fragrance;
      An old man's indulgence is all the more a fanatic
         passion.

嫩蕊輕盈風味重。白頭痴戀益情濃。

叢芳中。任他蛺蝶弄。

入來香國訪嬌容。花底歡娛雲雨共。

臨覓桃源洞。老翁問跡踪。

JSGJ I.16a

* "Peach Blossom Cave" is a utopia. The term orig-
inated in the writings of Tao Qian of the Jin dynasty.
He depicts it as a secluded community of tranquility
and peace. In this rhyme, however, the term does not
carry the original connotation.
    † "Clouds and rain," see song 42.

TEN

Songs of Prodigals
and Addicts

The most unfortunate thing that could happen to an
affluent Cantonese family was for its head or his son to
become addicted to one of the so-called four vices—that
is, womanizing among prostitutes (*piu*), compulsive
gambling (*dou*), excessive indulgence in food and drink
(*yam*), and smoking opium (*cheui*). Every one of these
vices, it was said, would bring ruin to a man and his
family—in the form of disease, failing health, loss of
wealth and property, sale of wife and children, and so
on—and unless the addict quickly repented, he was
doomed. One could avoid such vices by moral cultiva-
tion, according to Confucian teachings. Duty and re-
sponsibility to one's family must be placed above one's
individual interests. Not only could these vices destroy
the man, they could also cause the downfall of his entire
family.

It was known even back in China that the skewed
social environment of Chinatown encouraged the ram-
pant growth of the four vices. In the late nineteenth

century, one Cantonese writer, who was surnamed Yee
and a native of Sunwui county, wrote the following
couplet-poem based on what he had learned about
Chinatown life:

> Without a criminal conviction, he was exiled tens
>   of thousands of miles away;
> Married with a husband, she must maintain a life
>   of widowhood for eighteen years.
> To serve the parents,
> To take care of wife and children—
> One must realize the burden of family obligations;
> At a moment of crisis, who can shoulder such a
>   responsibility?
> To take a chance at the faantaan table,
> To womanize among prostitutes—
> Don't ever say this is the way it is in an overseas
>   stay;
> Once you kick the bucket, it's gone, never to return.
>
> So, be resolute to discipline yourself with virtues;
> Be aware of your behavior in the barbarian land.
> What kind of man does not entertain himself with the
>   joys of being with his parents, wife and children?
> What kind of man does not ever think of his own
>   family and the village home?

The Cantonese immigrants were well indoctrinated
with the moral teachings that encouraged family respon-
sibility. However, Chinatown's attitude toward these
vices, which were so dramatized in Cantonese folklore,
was quite ambivalent. Gambling and womanizing were
accepted as necessary evils by a population of desperate
men to whom escapist moments provided a remote
hope of becoming rich or fulfilling their physical needs.

At the same time, the four vices all were regarded as wicked and serious threats to a person's well-being. Opium in particular was singled out for attack, since the Cantonese immigrants' homeland had suffered dearly when the British importers of opium forced open the Chinese market to the drug. Numerous Chinatown vernacular rhymes ridiculed and cursed opium addicts; none showed any support for the drug, in contrast to their frequent toleration of gambling and womanizing.

In rhymes that exhort addicts to kick their bad habits, the wife plays a prominent role as an advice-giver, particularly in the case of gambling. In the rhymes of wealth ("Rhapsodies on Gold"), we saw the man express the desire for a concubine once he becomes rich. In these rhymes, the wife appears as wise and virtuous as the husband's gambling puts the family's finances in jeopardy. The attitude thus seems to be that a man needs a virtuous wife to support him through hard times; but when times are good, he prefers the companionship of a young woman as a reward for his success—a rather sad commentary indeed on traditional male and female roles.

192 I have been a bad boy ever since leaving home;
I should never, never have become so.
My parents reproached me in letter after
letter;
I must wake up and repent.
I must take notice of the wide and open road:
A straight avenue without obstacles.
Two years of frugality and hard work will bring
joyous success.
I can then easily turn around and go home in
splendid clothes.

出外唔好仔(一)。真真大不該。

雙親責罵信頻來。可在醒心快改悔。

覺路開。直前無阻磚(二)。

勤儉兩年歌滿載。翻身容易錦衣回。

(一)仔：兒子

(二)磚：作「磚」

JSGJ I.9b

193 A young man, lacking common sense;
By mistake, addicted to the four extremes.*
But suddenly he reforms his behavior and goes
straight;
Attribute it to an ancestral blessing.
Knowing what to do,
He redeems more than half of the family's fields
and gardens.
From now on, no more show of a reckless young
spender.
And no more worry about cold and hunger in
later years.

少年見識短。誤染四大端。
忽然改品業正門⁽一⁾。料必他們風水轉。
會打算⁽二⁾。田園贖返半。
自此唔冲闊亞官⁽三⁾。何愁日後受飢寒。

(一)
正門：正當職業，參看歌#116

(二)
冲：作「充」，參看歌#113

(三)
闊亞官：花錢很多的少爺

JSGJ I.8a

* "The four extremes" is another term for the four
major vices, mentioned in the introduction to this
section.

194 Gold and silver, all wastefully spent;
I look around, but no one appears to be my kin.
Who would take pity on a drifter overseas?
My memory is haunted by past extravagance—I am
  ashamed to show my face.
Alone in fright,
What a shabby prime of my life!
I'd better shape up and keep myself in line,
Make a new world for myself and ease my mind.

金銀散到盡。舉目似無親。

飄流海外有誰憐。憶惜化費唔敢認。

暗自驚。壯年這光景。

轉過章程立過品⁽一⁾。創翻世界方心平。

（一）
品：品德行爲

JSGJ I.8b

195 My life's half gone, but I'm still unsettled;
I've erred, I'm an expert at whoring and
gambling.
Syphilis almost ended my life.
I turned to friends for a loan, but no one took
pity on me.
Ashamed, frightened—
Now, I must wake up after this long nightmare;
Leap out of this misery and find my paradise.
But others laugh that old habits die hard and I'll
never change.

半生心未定。誤鍊賭燥精。

染成花柳幾喪命。遍借同僚莫一憐。

悔復驚。大夢從今醒。

跳出迷津登樂境。旁觀漫笑我油垱(一)。

（一）油垱：指「桐油垱」，四邑諺，

喻「死性不改」

JSGJ I.9a

196 Opium is most poisonous:
Ruining families, weakening the race.
Once you are addicted to it, your life is gone to waste;
Before the smoking lamp, you are constantly in a
daze.
O, strike the warning bell—
Shape up, don't be an addict to it anymore!
If you still cannot make this move,
You will sink deep into a bitter sea, and suffer endless
remorse!

破家兼弱種。最毒阿芙蓉(一)。
迷途一入萬緣空。癡對銀燈長在夢。
撞警鐘。沉沉還未總。
若果依然心不動。永淪黑海苦無窮。

（一）阿芙蓉‥Opium（鴉片）另一音譯

JSGJ I.1b

197 Shoulders, hunched up past his ears;
Haggard and thin, a body wrapped with a layer of
skin.
No trace of an heroic air,
Only a withered and withdrawn look, just despicable.
His spirit is flat
As if he's about to drop dead.
He lazes away instead of taking care of the thousand
matters piled up in front of him;
All that knowledge and all those ideas, abandoned.

肩頭高過耳。瘦削得層皮。(一)

全無半點英雄氣。形像衰頹眞可鄙。

神情癡。儼然就將死。

萬事到頭都懶理。經綸滿腹也拋離。

（一）得：剩下

JSGJ II.49b

198　Holding the bamboo pipe in his hands,
　　　Paying tribute to the white-haired clans,
　　　He pawns away his shirts and trousers, but it's still
　　　　　not enough;
　　　So, he gives up his land and garden, and sells the
　　　　　family mansion.
　　　All for this poisonous addiction.
　　　Wife and children cry, day and night.
　　　O, turn back before it's too late for the happiness
　　　　　that might lie ahead of you!
　　　Otherwise, a piece of wood is smarter than you!

手拿一碌竹⁽一⁾。進貢白頭族。
典⁽二⁾褲當衣供不足。化盡田園又賣屋。
染此毒。妻孥日夜哭。
趁早回頭還有福。不然笨過個條木⁽三⁾。

（一）一碌：一枝
（二）典當：典押
（三）個：那；參看歌 #111

JSGJ I.2b

199 For five measly milligrams, he argues and weighs;
   Then he lies down sidewise, feet curled up like a
      shrimp,
   With his bamboo pipe over a lamp lit next to his
      head.
   His face, like a bird's; his body, like an insect's;
   His eyelids, in constant recess.
   Outside the house, he fears the sweeping wind;
   Not only will his wife and children suffer from
      cold and hunger,
   He will drop dead before King Yimlo calls his
      number.*

五厘必爭賤。點着則頭燈(一)。

橫床直竹腳丁騰。(二)面似鵲形身似螽。

眼撐撐。出門怕風猛。

不獨妻兒捱飢冷。閻王夫請佢先行。

（一）
　則：作「側」

（二）
　風猛：風大

JSGJ I.1b

*King Yimlo (Yanluo Wang), the ruler of the underworld in popular Chinese mythology, keeps a registry of deeds on all the mortals. The soul of the deceased must appear before his court. King Yimlo's verdict on the deceased's deeds in the mortal world, as recorded in the registry, will determine the fate of the soul—to be punished or rewarded, to be reincarnated into either animal or human life, etc.

200 The filthy poison brings you ruin:
It drains away life's very essence.
It makes your head look like a dead man's,
   and your face, too.
And your shrugged shoulders, hunched back,
   with your waist bent.
You are a good-for-nothing,
A nightmare in your family's geomantic display.*
Your family fortune, all gone up in smoke,
   What can you live on?
You will suffer pain, cold, and hunger in your
   old age!

穢毒貽害爾。檀吸丹田氣。（一）

頭如魁佬面如而。腰曲背駝肩聳起。

冇作置（二）。人呼風水尾。

吹盡家財無所倚。老來受苦抵寒飢。

（一）檀：作「擅」

（二）冇作置：沒有作為

JSGJ I.1a

*In popular Cantonese belief, geomantic considera-
tions affect the fortunes of all family members. Thus,
sites for building construction or burial are seriously
regarded so that a decision will not jeopardize the
family fortune. Cf. song 193.

201 The taxed gum is actually a poison.*
Don't ever take it as some kind of elixir pill.
Get away from it, otherwise misfortune will
    come:
Home ruined, property lost, and relatives all in
    shame.
Humiliation will haunt you all your life.
So, why not turn back now?
Look, a longtime addiction will wither your ability
    to sire;
Your wife will cry and cry, with much complaint!

公膠原係毒。勿作靈丹服。
若不湔除是非福。傾家蕩產玷親屬。
終身辱。還弗回頭速。
食久枯精無孕育。常累妻房多怨哭。

JSGJ I.1b

*The import of opium was taxed before it was
banned altogether by the U.S. government in 1909.

202 The taxed gum is a tremendous burden:*
   Once addicted to it, it does you in:
   Pockets empty, clothes ragged,
   Furniture pawned, children sold...
   All for smoking opium.
   Indulgence shows no concern for the future:
   Talent and abilities all go down the gutter.
   No way to escape from it, even if you put on
      wings!

公膠真大累。練熟人睇虛(一)。
囊空如洗衣藍褸。家私典埋賣仔女(四)。
定工吹。痴迷無遠慮。
一身本事付流水。縱然插翼也難飛。

（一）睇：或作「體」
（二）藍：作「襤」
（三）典埋：都典押了
（四）仔女：子女

JSGJ I.1a

* "Taxed gum," see song 201.

203 Face haggard, turning yellow and puffy,
Waist, bent like a drawn bow.
Lying on his side next to a small lit lamp,
He holds the pipe as his family fortune goes
down its hole.
Look at him:
Soon he will be six feet underground.
Lazy, remiss, he won't move even if you drag
him.
He's about to meet King Yimlo at Hell's tenth
palace.*

面已變黃腫。腰似一枝弓。

側身點着小燈籠。扛起家財過斗孔。

看形容(一)。就入埋人塚。

懈性懶情拖不動。將會閻王十殿宮。

（一）形容：容貌外表

JSGJ II.48b

* According to Chinese popular belief, hell has eigh-
teen "palaces" where the dead person's mortal deeds
are reviewed. The eighteenth palace hands out the most
severe punishments. King Yimlo, see song 199.

204 The aroma of taxed gum, a fragrance appealing
    to the nostrils.*
A puff of it surely livens up the soul.
But once you're addicted, your face becomes
    a layer of black skin;
Take it often, and your shoulders become shrugged
    and thin.
You're held captive by this devil—
Organs ruined by opium poison.
It retails for over thirty dollars a tin can;
Kick the habit and don't ever hesitate, my dear
    friend.

公膏香撲鼻。吒口壯神氣。
練成大癮面烏皮。食得多來肩聳起。
被魔痴。鴉毒深攻裏。
每罐價銀沽卅幾。勸君早戒勿遲疑。

JSGJ II.49b

* "Taxed gum," see song 201.

205 I plead with you, Husband, have some self-control:
Don't ever go to a place to gamble.
Faantaan is the worst, driving a person to poverty;
And keep away from paaigau and bullfights, too.
Hurry and wake up—
Please listen to your wife's remonstrations.
If you are still fanatic about this, like a dreamer,
Everything—our house and fields—will all become
    nothing.

誠郎須自重。勿入博塲中。

番攤最易累人窮。牌九鬥牛都莫弄。

猛惺忪。聽從奴勸奉。

若是癡迷仍在夢。樓房田地總成空。

JSGJ II.7a

206 I am holding several beans,*

Husband, can you guess how many there are
exactly?

Even a great man, once into the game, will
lower his head in defeat;

A rare lucky moment might yield a winner or
two.

But if you knock on lady luck's door too often;

If you bet on one slot, take your chances on the other
three,

You will lose all your gold and silver, and be left
empty-handed.

I pray, dear man, don't ever fancy this game again!

奴揸幾粒荳。請郎汝咕(一)透。
英雄入局料垂頭。好彩(二)有時中兩口。
倘多叩。買一開三湊。
輸去金銀空拍手。願君棄此勿癡謀。

(一) 咕 : 作「估」

(二) 好彩 : 好運氣

JSGJ II.7a

 *In an improvised faantaan game, beans are used in-
stead of coins as the game apparatus. See introduction
("Chinatown Low Life" section) for a description of
the game.

207 Greed never makes wishes come true,
I've been losing for more than three years straight.
For all this, tears flood my wife's eyes.
Ashamed, how can I ever face her again?
I must reform right away;
I must correct my mistakes, change for the better.
My wishful thinking in the past has truly brought
    me humiliation;
From now on, to all my wife's words I must
    faithfully listen.

貪心不遂願。輪落三幾年。

累及拙荊悲連連。問心無顏相見面。

即刻(一)變。改過而遷善。

前日想頭眞討賤。從今盡聽老婆(二)言。

（一）即刻：參看歌
#112

（二）老婆：妻子

JSGJ II.6b

208 She's truly a wonderful wife,
  Always around to point out my errors.
  When I lose money in a game of chance, whom
    can I blame?
  As I think of it, I'm afraid it's all my fault.
  I've made mistakes.
  From now on, my dear mate,
  I won't enter any house of chance again or cause
    any more trouble;
  We may be poor, but no more of this suffering
    and struggle.

真係好老婆。時常糾我過。

博錢輸去耐誰何。想起翻來唔得妥。

自己錯。從今好內助。

不入偏門終免禍。雖窮唔駛受折磨。

(一)老婆：參看歌 #207

(二)耐：作「奈」

(三)偏門：不正當行業，指賭博；
  參看歌 #116

(四)唔駛：參看歌 #113

JSGJ II.6b

ELEVEN

Songs of the Hundred Men's Wife

Many outstanding Chinese literary works have movingly depicted the romance between a young scholar and a prostitute. The woman is inevitably beautiful, virtuous, talented in the arts and music, and sometimes also in literature, all of which makes her a perfect companion for the scholar. Usually the affair concludes in tragedy, as societal attitudes toward prostitutes prevent a happy union between the two. Although sympathy was frequently expressed toward the woman, prostitution was also strongly condemned by Confucian morality, which held that such indulgence would only lead to a life of poverty, humiliation, and moral decadence. The fine line between acceptance and condemnation of prostitution was based on a judgment of intent: was it love or lust? A distinction was also made between "high-class" and "low-class" prostitutes. The former, euphemistically called "courtesans," were trained to entertain elite patrons; the latter offered "no frills" service.

Prostitution was a social institution in old China. In

the Pearl River delta during the late nineteenth century, brothels were seen in many urban centers as international trade brought affluence to some segments of the population. Young men were constantly exhorted to avoid prostitutes, and venereal diseases became a major concern.

The Cantonese were extremely cynical in the terminology they used for prostitutes. They called these women *lougeui*, meaning "always holding [her legs] up." A brothel was called *lougeui jaai*, meaning "lougeui camp." A name that was more reserved, but equally insulting, was *baak haak chai*, "hundred men's wife." Actually, the term "hundred men's wife" reflected the chauvinistic attitude of Cantonese men toward such women.

Prostitution was a necessity in the early history of the state of California, as we have seen. It satisfied the needs of the "married but single" Chinese men who were recruited to work in the West. Some Caucasian politicians and local newspapers even advocated allowing Chinese prostitutes, rather than wives, to immigrate, so that the status quo could be maintained and a massive Asian settlement could be avoided. Chinese prostitutes would also act as an effective deterrent to Chinese men's going to white prostitutes, and would thus maintain so-called Caucasian racial purity. Hence, prostitution thrived in Chinatown's bachelor society.

In the early days, some Chinese women came voluntarily to work as prostitutes, regarding prostitution as a way to earn a living without much capital investment. Later, however, as criminal elements in the community took control of this profitable venture it became a major vice. Women were sold, kidnapped, tricked, and forced into the profession. As mentioned in the general introduction, these women lived a most inhumane existence in Chinatown. Chinatown's community newspapers frequently reported on the escapes of young prostitutes. They covered Tong wars over territorial disputes or over the right of ownership of a prostitute, and told of Donaldina Cameron's numerous rescues of "slave girls" from houses of ill repute and the halfway house where these women were rehabilitated before returning to a normal life. Numerous editorials and other writings called for action against this vice in Chinatown. Both the prostitutes and their customers were satirized and ridiculed. However, these efforts failed to eradicate prostitution so long as racism prevented the majority of Chinese men from having a normal family life in the United States.

In my research I came across a news item in the 1908 *Chung Sai Yat Po* that tells of an older prostitute named Ah Gam ("Goldie"), who was rescued and placed in the halfway house. Several days later, there was further news of Goldie. She had been found insane and diseased, her eyesight failing and her skin rotting away. She could not stay at the halfway house but was sent to a mental institution at Napa, California. The headline read: "An End to the Life of Another Prostitute." Nothing ever appeared about her again.

209　What a street-walking broad:
　　　All dolled up like a charming young lass,
　　　Like a native-born from Canada,
　　　Loitering on the streets day and night.
　　　I follow her from behind,
　　　Thinking she might be something nice.
　　　Quickly I walk up to take a good look:
　　　O, my, is she a wilted flower!

恁個老舉妞(一)。扮成似嬌娃。

恰如土生在加拿(二)。朝夕時常隨街耍(二)。

尾跟他。祇估好貨(三)也。

急步上前睇一吓(四)。細看原底是殘花。

（四）睇吓：參看歌#120
（三）好貨：正當的好東西
（二）隨街耍：在街上遊蕩
（一）老舉妞：妓女

JSGJ II.19a

210 Yes, it tickles my funny bone to tell you:
The fashion now is Western.
We in this business of pleasing men must keep
up with the trend.
Our dresses must be new and in style.
Even if we have to sell and pawn,
We'll buy all the clothes we want.
Doll ourselves up like beautiful American-borns;
Surely the men will find us very pleasant.

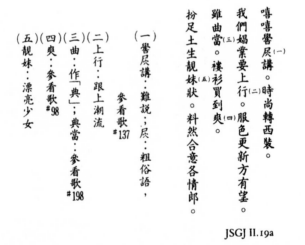

嘻嘻譽屄講〔一〕。時尚轉西裝。

我們娼業要上行〔二〕。服色更新方有望。

雖曲當〔三〕。襪衫買到爽〔四〕。

扮足土生靚妹狀〔五〕。料然合意各情郎。

（一）譽屄講：難説；屄：粗俗語，
　　參看歌 #137

（二）上行：跟上潮流

（三）曲：作「典」；典當：參看歌 #198

（四）爽：參看歌 #98

（五）靚妹：漂亮少女

JSGJ II.19a

211 Trying to line up fun-loving johns,
They've changed their clothing styles.
Now they wear heels in whorehouses
Like the fad among school girls,
As if there's no longer a difference between the two.
Still, their skin and flesh are for hire.
If they don't follow the trends, people will be
   bored
And they might as well close up shop and take
   down their signs.

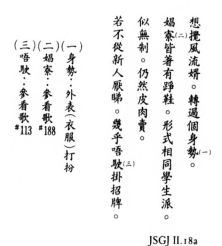

想攬風流婿。轉過個身勢。

娼寮皆著有蹺鞋。形式相同學生派(一)。

似無制。仍然皮肉賣。

若不從新人厭睇(三)。幾乎唔駛掛招牌。

（一）身勢：外表（衣服）打扮

（二）娼寮：參看歌 #188

（三）唔駛：參看歌 #113

JSGJ II.18a

212 The whore has changed her appearance:
Now she looks just like a cute young lass.
Her look and her attire are indeed impressive;
Her behavior no longer reveals her lowly identity.
She leads her john by the hand;
Together they go out to eat at a restaurant.
Everyone marvels at her beauty and her social graces;
Who dares to say she is just a prostitute by trade!

老舉變容像。儼若嫩姑娘。

渾身打扮確排塲。舉動不同專制樣。

挈阿相[一]。齊飲茶樓上[二]。

彼美在行人讚賞。乜誰敢話佢當娼

（一）阿相：老相好

（二）乜誰：什麼人

JSGJ II.18a

213 The john looks smart and swell;
The whore finds him to her liking.
Bound together by clouds and rain, they are
inseparable;*
She wants to sleep with him, so she even pays his
bills.
What a fanatic indulgence in passion!
All for a young man with a handsome face.
She loves him from the very bottom of her heart;
For her, not even gold is more precious than a good
young man.

嫖客生秀氣。妓女甚投機。
綢繆雲雨不相離。倒貼賬銀甘與寢。
情戀癡。子弟姿容美。
愛佢猶如心肝蒂。黃金那及好男兒。

JSGJ II.24a

*"Clouds and rain," see song 42.

214 The visitor is truly a handsome young man;
   A prostitute sizes him up out of the corner of her
      eye.
   The look of a rich young lad, a most pleasing
      sight;
   Right away, she sends him her regards through the
      talking wire.*
   In her soft and sensuous voice,
   She invites him to drop by.
   He is a passionate soul indeed, and slick.
   She lets him have his way, and doesn't want to pull up
      her panties for even a short while.

遊子真美貌。妓女眼角勾⁽¹⁾。
闊少模樣遂心頭。即打喊線去問候⁽²⁾。
咩咩嘍。請他來寒口⁽³⁾。
果係情濃兼滑漏⁽⁴⁾。任佢風流褲不抽⁽⁵⁾。

（五）抽：穿上
（四）滑漏：油滑順意
（三）寒口：妓院
（二）喊線：電話
（一）闊少：有錢少爺

JSGJ II.23b

*"The talking wire"—the telephone.

215 Born with a fine and gentle air,
Predestined in life to be intimate with women.
Young and handsome, he's perfect, without a
flaw;
O, what prostitute won't want to have some
fun with him?
Passionately loving him,
Emotions bound like lacquer and glue.*
The pimp hears about this, and scolds and beats
her up.
She runs off and sneaks back to China with her
lover.

生得丰儀雅。命裡帶桃花(一)。
青春貌美更無瑕。妓婦相見同樂耍。
愛戀他。情如膠漆也。
龜鴇聞知來打罵。私逃密約返中華。

（一）桃花：指「桃花運」，受女人喜歡
的男子曰有桃花命

JSGJ II.23b

* "Lacquer and glue," see song 44.

216 A word of advice for you, dear *peipa* girl:*
Best to find a good man and get hitched to him.
Get out of this business while there's still time to
reach paradise;
The gaiety of pleasure houses in the past, where
is it now?
You want respect, don't you?
Then, shack up together and hope for a son.
In a blink, a flower will wither and then no man will
care;
Who in this world wants to pluck a wilted plum
branch?

諫汝琵琶妹⁽一⁾。好佬跟翻個⁽二⁾。
回頭趁早上蓬萊。楚館繁華今安在⁽三⁾。
欲貴哉。住埋望生仔⁽五⁾。
轉瞬花殘人不愛。有誰貪折老枝梅。

(五)(四)(三)(二)(一)
生　住　跟　佬　琵
仔　埋　翻　：　琶
：　：　：　男　妹
生　同　跟　子　：
兒　居　隨　　　參
子　，　　　　　看
　　一　　　　　歌
　　齊　　　　　#131
　　居
　　住

JSGJ II.28b

*"*Peipa* girl," see song 131.

217 A green mansion is a place of filth and shame,*
Of lost chastity and lost virtue.
Most repulsive is it to kiss the customers on the
lips
And let them fondle every part of my body.
I hesitate, I resist;
All the more ashamed, beyond words.
I must by all means leave this troupe of flowers
and rouge;
Find a nice man and follow him as his woman.

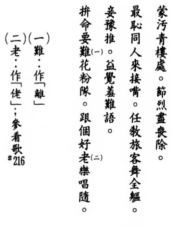

蒙污青樓處。節烈盡喪除。
最恥同人來接嘴。任教旅客舞全軀。
妾豫推(一)。益覺羞難語。
拼命要難花粉隊。跟個好老樂唱隨(二)。

(二)(一)
老難
：：
作作
「「
佬離
」」
：；
參
看
歌
#216

JSGJ I.21a

*A "green mansion" is a brothel.

218 Hitching up with a nice young man—
This whore sure has good vision.
Suddenly she quits her profession and her prayers
are answered;
Rids herself of the infamous label and becomes his
second wife.
It's a big deal for her:
She wanders the streets no more.
Now she retires to learn the manners of a family
woman;
She's spared from being flesh and skin for hire.

跟個佳子弟。老舉好眼界（一）。
忽然上岸遂心懷。換却臭名稱二奶（二）。
咁架勢（三）。再唔蕩落街（四）。
而今歸學家人禮。免將皮肉作生涯。

（一）眼界：眼光見識
（二）二奶：參看歌 #160
（三）架勢：威風
（四）蕩落街：在街上遊蕩

JSGJ I.21b

219 Prostitution ruins the body most harmfully.
Come ashore, the sooner the better.
My advice is to get hitched to a man, and don't
    ever forget, dear young lass:
It's no shame to have a decent meal with plain tea.
All in all—
You'd also gain a husband.
We've all witnessed the frequent raids of brothels
    in the Golden Gate;
You need not worry about these roughnecks once
    you live with a man.

為娼最賤體。上岸速更佳。
勉嬌跟老莫忘懷(一)。淡飯清茶唔失禮。
講極細(二)。都添有夫婿。
眼見金門常搜寨。住埋唔怕佢蠻嚟(三)。

（一）老：作「佬」。參看歌 #216
（二）細：作「哂」：講極哂：說到底
（三）嚟：來

JSGJ II.27b

220 The sufferings in a Cheun tower are unbearable.*
     To leave it is to be spared from sorrow.
     To be a prostitute is to be dirt cheap, and worse.
     Today, happily, I've met a fine young man.
     I vow to eternity;
     I will withstand even poverty.
     The domestic life may lack the luster of the gay
          quarters;
     But it's far better than living in a green mansion
          as a hundred men's wife!†

秦樓苦譽捱⁽⁻⁾。別却免愁懷。

為娼一件賤過坭。今日幸逢佳子弟。

盟海誓。貪窮都要抵⁽²⁾。

住家雖則無常禮。勝作青樓百客妻。

（二）（一）
抵：：譽捱：：難捱
忍受；；參看歌#10

JSGJ II.21a

*"Cheun (Qin) tower" is a brothel.
†"Green mansion," see song 217.